AT HOME IN NATURE

ROB WOOD

AT
A LIFE OF
HOME
UNKNOWN MOUNTAINS
IN
AND DEEP WILDERNESS
NATURE

RMB

RMB | Rocky Mountain Books Ltd.
rmbooks.com
@rmbooks
facebook.com/rmbooks

Cataloguing data available from Library and Archives Canada
ISBN 9781771602501 (paperback)
ISBN 9781771602518 (electronic)

Printed and bound in Canada by Friesens

Distributed in Canada by Heritage Group Distribution
and in the US by Publishers Group West

For information on purchasing bulk quantities of this book, or to
obtain media excerpts or invite the author to speak at an event,
please visit rmbooks.com and select the "Contact Us" tab.

RMB | Rocky Mountain Books is dedicated to the environment and
committed to reducing the destruction of old-growth forests. Our books
are produced with respect for the future and consideration for the past.

We acknowledge the financial support of the Government of Canada
through the Canada Book Fund and the Canada Council for the Arts,
and of the province of British Columbia through the British Columbia
Arts Council and the Book Publishing Tax Credit.

For Jennie, Sarah and Ashley

CONTENTS

ACKNOWLEDGMENTS

FOR EDITING AND ENCOURAGEMENT:
Judith Wright, Catherine Rubinger, Richard Wood

FOR ESSENTIAL TIMELY SERVICES
PROVIDED IN FARAWAY PLACES:
Canadian Health Care
Canadian Coast Guard

FOR THEIR LOVING SUPPORT:
Laurie and Kiersten

INTRODUCTION

THE SHORT WINTER DAY IS fading fast. A swirling blizzard chills our faces and buffets every step. Exhausted, we slog slowly up through steep virgin forest. Deep, heavy, fresh snow sticks and balls up the climbing skins on our skis and slows us down even more. Our goal is a tiny alpine cabin 4,000 ft. above the ocean in our local coastal mountains. With this unusually deep snow pack the cabin could be buried. With no marked trail, it would be hard to find in broad daylight, maybe impossible in darkness and this snowstorm.

"Don't fancy a night out without shelter in this." The thought drives us on.

"Not everybody's idea of a perfect birthday party."

Just as darkness closes in, there are signs of the cabin's position. The slope eases and the snow-loaded trees become smaller and more widely spaced. Headlamps, however, show nothing but undulating snow humps, any one of which may conceal the cabin. At first, as the six of us set to panicky searching, our probing reveals nothing.

"Must be 'round here somewhere," I mutter in frustration.

"Remember that gnarly old yellow cedar snag that stands right in front of the cabin?" my wife, Laurie, thinks aloud.

"Right now the trees all look the same," I grumble.

"Yeah, but the cabin tree is bigger with no foliage ... like that one over there."

In the lee of the big dead cedar snag, the wind has scooped out a depression in the surface of the snow. A few stabs at the snow face with a shovel reveal the distinctive triangular gable atop the front wall of the cabin.

"Eureka! We've got it!"

In pools of headlamp light, digging starts right away. Without discussion, someone clears the chimney top. Someone else chops down into the hard compacted snow pack while others shovel out the loosened snow and cut back a ramp for steps. About four feet down, the roof of the porch appears. Another eight feet down, and finally, "Bingo!" – the cabin door. The whole group and their bulky packs squeeze into the 8 × 16 ft. cabin and ceremoniously shut the door, closing out the weather and the night.

Bic lighters busily light the white gas lamp, the propane cooker and the wood stove. A big stainless steel kettle, stuffed full of snow, melts on the stove for a "brew" of tea. One end of the tiny cabin is a general work space and cooking area where each body must now slide tactfully around the others to find enough personal space to strip off wet clothing and hang it from nails in the rafters. At the other end is a sleeping loft and tucked below it a plywood table with benches on either side which will be the centre of the evening eating and lounging. Then later the table will drop down flush with the benches to form another sleeping platform. The whole arrangement is compact and functional. In next to no time it is also warm and cozy. All the wet clothes are hanging up in the rafters to dry.

Very soon the master wilderness cook, Laurie, whips up what seems to us like a gourmet meal of curried chicken, complete with stewed fruit "cobbler" for dessert.

After dinner the conversation turns to the question, "How did this all come about?"

Laurie and I had decided to celebrate my 60th birthday by inviting a few younger outdoorsy friends to one of our favorite places on the coast, this funky old alpine cabin that had been built many years ago by some old-timers. It is in a remote area on the mainland, at the back of a small inlet not far from our home in the Discovery Islands.

After a three-hour ride in our 33 foot catamaran, *Quintano*, there was normally a six-hour hike from the beach, on old logging roads, then up a rugged trail through virgin old-growth forest to alpine meadows and wonderful open skiing and hiking slopes. On this occasion, as expected, the trail was invisible, buried deep in the snow pack, so we had to feel our way up the mountain, trying to stay on the crest of a subtle ridge. Although there had been bad weather forecast, we had set out anyway because trips like this take a lot of planning, it's hard to get everyone together at short notice and, if the opportunity is not taken, there is a danger of not being able to reschedule, or of never going at all. Also, it's possible to have a good time even in bad weather. Besides, the forecasts are not always correct. Today had been a long, tough day typical of "bushwhacking" in the Coast Range wilderness and, as usual, remarkably rewarding, especially after finding the security of the cabin.

Most of us are stripped down to our thermal underwear, hunkered onto a spot on a bench, with a mug of hot sweet tea and a big contented smile. What relief. Sheer luxury.

"You notice we invited a few apprentices along to help carry our loads, as well as breaking trail, doing most of the digging and making the tea."

"You must have learned a few tricks over the years, eh?"

"Well, you young guys do get a few benefits, like boat rides and being shown where the cabin is even in the dark, not to mention Laurie's cooking."

"We'll buy that. After all the proof is in the pudding ... and the stew."

As we all subside into a long winter evening of relaxed and relieved euphoria, attention comes round to my birthday. After the usual congratulations, and sensing I am suitably primed for storytelling, some of the "youths" start asking questions, mainly about our alternative lifestyle....

"What made you chose to leave the mainstream and come to live on a remote island on the BC coast?" "How and when did you find a place to settle down?" "When and where did you two meet? ... Was it love at first sight?" "How did you get started living on raw land?" "What's your homestead and community like now?"

"That's a lot of questions and a long story," I reply.

"Let's have it. We've got all night."

"And all next day tomorrow, unless the weather improves."

"All right, you asked for it," I grin and settle back on the bench, back against the cabin wall.

"How about another brew to wet my whistle?"

"More cobbler, anyone?"

I

LEAVING THE OLD COUNTRY

**"What made you choose to leave the
old country and come to Canada?"**

MY PASSION FOR FREEDOM GOES back to my
memories of earliest childhood, when I felt happi-
est outdoors, growing up in a picturesque English
village that nestled into the edge of the Yorkshire
moors. Roaming freely for days at a time in the
nearby woods, fields and open moors gave me a
deep and lasting sense of nature's timeless flow, in

which everything made sense and fitted together. The village felt as if it belonged in the landscape, and I felt as if I belonged to them both. The lifestyle of the villagers probably hadn't changed much in hundreds of years. The milk was still being delivered by horse and cart every day, though the first black and white TV and the odd motor car had already shown up.

When, at the tender age of eleven, I had to leave the beautiful village on the edge of the wild moors and move to the suburbs of a big city, I wept for days. It seemed that an essential part of myself was being left behind. Had I but known how true this would turn out to be, the crying would have been even longer and harder. My previous freedom to explore the wonders of the natural world was curtailed sharply amid the new constraints at home, and especially at the city high school (though, according to my two big brothers and two bigger sisters, I was spoiled and allowed to be rebellious).

I performed just well enough at school to get by, living for the only enjoyable part, which was playing rugby. Even better were the exciting weekends away on the fells and crags deep in the remote countryside, sharing rambling adventures and camaraderie with my working-class pals. My parents had introduced us to family camping and walking holidays in the mountains, and Dad even had a couple of us doing a bit of easy rock climbing. He had an old climbing rope hanging up in the garage. In my class at school there were a couple of pals, Wilber and Polly, Boy Scouts who liked messing about with ropes and knots and had done some camping. So one sunny spring day, bored and frustrated to death in French class, gazing longingly out of the window and thinking about the local cliffs where I had seen people rock climbing with ropes, I had a flash of inspiration that would change my life. A quickly scribbled note passed across the classroom to the Boy Scouts said, "Do you want to go rock climbing with me this weekend? I have a rope and we could ride our bikes to the crag."

Fortunately for us, that very first day at the crag, there was an older climber making fast and graceful ascents of fierce-looking overhanging cracks – without ropes. Obviously he was an expert, and seeing us "young 'uns" trying to figure out how to get started, he took us under his wing and showed us how to use the rope properly. His name was Tom, and his shocking white hair and beard made him look a lot older than his athletic ability suggested.

His old-fashioned teaching method was direct and to the point. "You tie yourself on to the rope like this," and with a few deft twists and turns of the rope he had it secured round his waist. Then, after deliberately pausing to make sure his audience was paying attention, he took an end of the rope and demonstrated again in slow motion: "The rabbit comes up through the rabbit hole, round the back of the tree for a pee and then back down the hole again."

With a grin and a mirthless chuckle he continued. "That's a bowline, and it's the best knot in the world, but don't forget, it needs an extra half hitch for good measure." He paused again for maximum theatrical effect before switching his facial expression, rolling his eyes in exaggerated sternness and delivering his final apocalyptic message in broad Yorkshire dialect to his now fully attentive young audience:

"'Cos yer life might depend on it!"

We all gasped in astonishment – before rolling on the ground laughing with relief.

Besides learning to use the rope to protect ourselves, we were deeply impressed by Tom's artistic, graceful movement on the rock, which made difficulty and danger look like an easy dance. Right from the start the old sorcerer had taught his apprentices that climbing was about a lot more than Boy Scouts playing with ropes. With a bit of practice, this informative and inspiring introduction enabled us right away to do a few easy but, to us, hugely impressive real climbs. Seeing us arrive home so dirty, tired out but animated and ebullient, our parents must have wondered what on earth had got into us. Little did they know what this was to be the start of.

Climbing was so much fun it quickly became an addiction, taking us out to crags on the nearby grit stone edges in all kinds of weather every weekend. A unique characteristic of the local "grit stone" rock was wind-eroded vertical and horizontal cracks which were smooth and lacking in distinctive micro-features to pull up on. Sensing our enthusiasm, the older guys showed us a specialized technique of "jamming" fists and toes into the cracks. It was painful and took lots of nerve and balance, as well as upper body strength. It meant learning to stay cool and trust our own grip, especially when hanging out on these "jams" 30 or 40 feet above the ground.

The only price for these initiation rites was being what the older guys called the "brew boys." In other words, the apprentices had to make the tea and carry all the gear. Needless to say, there was a Catch-22 involved. The ropes had to be coiled just right, and of course the tea had to be perfect. As with climbing itself, failure had serious consequences. An imperfect "brew" accrued so many penalty points, which meant having to make so many more brews.

There was one young apprentice climber called Ginger Dick who was taking his turn to make the brew for some very famous master climbers in a tent after dark. The responsibility was making Dick flustered and he spilled the candle into the billy of boiling brew.

"Never mind," he thought. "They won't notice."

When the most famous rock climber in the

country sipped his tea, his teeth immediately stuck together and he almost choked before spurting scalding tea all over his sleeping bag. Ginger Dick had to make the next 25 brews for that mistake.

Hitchhiking took us rebellious young teenagers farther afield with overnight camping to even more remote and beautiful fells and crags. These adventures reinforced my childhood sense of being at home in the wilds and led to highly valued lifelong friendships, especially with my buddies Wilber and Polly and the master climber, Tom, whom we had met that first day at the local crag. The more I experienced this mysterious hidden connectivity, the more convinced I became of the presence in wild places of a vital component of life that urban existence was missing and possibly even precluding. This mystery induced in me a lifelong quest for explanation and meaning.

HAVING MADE IT THROUGH HIGH school, I was accepted by a prestigious school of architecture in London for an arduous five-year training program. What was particularly unusual about this course was that students were expected to follow their own path. The difficulty for me at the time, however, was finding a path that was comfortable enough to stay on. There was no problem learning about the history of art and architecture, but the more I studied urban society the more it seemed to me that the contemporary man-made environment was increasingly separating people from nature and from each other. Even though I wanted to believe in science and reason, their application to planning and urban management policies invariably seemed to lead to an oppressive, superficial and ultimately soulless monoculture that stifled free creativity and standardized or omitted vital components of life.

"Little boxes made of ticky-tacky and they all look just the same," sang Pete Seeger.

Five years' training as an architect did nothing to allay my early doubts about the veracity of the prevalent "cosmology" of modern society. It promoted the notion that because we are separate and superior, humans have the right and the ability to dominate and abuse the rest of the world without any risk to ourselves. While accounting for untold damage to the environment and other cultures, this dangerously deluded myth thrived on the fact that most of our thinking and behaviour was not actually conscious but rather automatic replaying of subconscious cultural conditioning (propaganda). Both as individuals and collectively, we all suffered from delusions of our own self-importance, which we then self-righteously imposed, often violently, on others. Most of us were busy pulling the wool over our own eyes and those of our children, perpetuating tunnel vision. Ironically, conscious brain power, the very attribute that was supposed to make us separate and superior in the first place, was exactly what we rarely practised.

Eventually, in my final design thesis I proposed an alternative global settlement pattern of largely self-sufficient villages, pockets of low rise, high density housing with enough population to support the facilities of daily life within walking distance. Density would be alleviated by generous access to public green space and surrounding local food-producing gardens and farms. Intermediate technologies would be powered by renewable energy. Electric cars would connect villages on small roads feeding into regional motorways with electromagnetic belts so that all the cars travelled at the same speed, like trains. Each village would have unique specialty products expressed in organic architecture evolving from its local ecosystem.

Meanwhile, at least once a month, I would escape the intense intellectual pressure, the hectic pace and the squalor of low income life in London by hitchhiking up to the mountains. The relative sanity, sincerity and humour of my working-class mates, along with the peace and beauty of the remote countryside, were the perfect antidote. I made friends with Stevey Smith, who had a house in Windermere at the heart of the Lake District National Park, which had become a favourite meeting place for climbers. As well as becoming another lifelong friend and fellow adventurer, he shared with me his passion for folk music. So, after many happy days spent tramping around the hills and scaring ourselves to death on the crags, we would invariably end up singing our hearts out in a local pub. We shared the thrill of another form of hidden connectivity which we lovingly referred to as "magic," the authentic traditional folk music of people whose remote rural lifestyle and culture were still grounded in the vernacular of their local environment. Even the old pubs invariably looked and felt as if they belonged in their landscape, especially after a few pints of local ale.

It was becoming more and more difficult for me to keep a comfortable balance between social experience and natural experience, and probably impossible for me ever to be remotely happy in London or in any other big city. Furthermore, the encroachment of the soulless monoculture into the beloved countryside of my native land was alarming and in sharp contrast to the authentic sincerity of what was being sacrificed.

The only hope was in knowing that lots of other folks shared my disenchantment with the "system." At that time, in the mid-1960s, a tremendous surge of "alternative consciousness" was inspiring young people around the world with love and peace. Protest demonstrations in the streets of London against the Vietnam War were all the rage. So too were listening all night long to Bob Dylan and Joan Baez singing "The Times They Are a-Changin'." Pubs, coffee shops, books and magazines and especially street theatre were loudly and colourfully promoting the "counterculture," and the emancipation of women, blacks, students and colonies. The word "environment" was the latest buzz.

In the midst of all this upheaval while working on our projects in the middle of the night, smoking cigarettes, drinking black coffee and listening to Gordon Lightfoot's "Canadian Railroad Trilogy," a Canadian flatmate asked me casually, "Wanna go to Expo 67 in Montreal this summer?"

"What the hell for? There's no mountains there, are there?"

"Well actually, yes there are, and it would also be fun and it might change the world."

It also just happened that both my big sisters were living in Montreal at the time and raving about Expo 67. So (with apologies to Ian and Sylvia), "Out on runway number nine, the jet plane that I was leaving on, not knowing when I'd be back again," was heading not south to the Alps but west to new horizons.

Trudeaumania and Expomania offered exciting and hopeful times, full of promise for a better world. The Beatles' *Sergeant Pepper* album was released the day I arrived in Montreal, and later that night I had my first toke of marijuana. Welcome to Canada!

ALLEGIANCE TO NATURE

**"Why did you choose to come
to the BC west coast?"**

AFTER WORKING IN MONTREAL ALL winter and
then spending the summer climbing in the Rockies,
I just had to make a pilgrimage to the rock climbers' Mecca, Yosemite Valley in sunny California.
After I'd spent a few weeks of soaking up the
staggeringly powerful natural ambience of "the
Valley" and the equally powerful social vibrations

of the hippie movement at its peak, a synchronicity occurred which resulted in the most extraordinary experience of my life.

In Camp 4, the climbers' campground in Yosemite, seemingly quite by chance, I met an old acquaintance from the Lake District climbing scene in the old country. Mick Burke had a reputation as a "hard" climber, with several significant ascents in the Alps and South America. He made it quite clear he was intending to climb the Nose of El Capitan, an approach to the summit which at that time was surrounded by an aura of impossibility. Only the very best local Yosemite climbers had succeeded in climbing this, the most famous and iconic rock climb in the world. The 3,000 ft. vertical granite wall took five days of supreme physical and psychological effort in the blazing, hundred-degree California sun.

Mick had already made seven false starts with different partners, all of whom had "psyched out" and had to "back off," so I was not altogether surprised when I noticed his beady eye focused on me. I had precious little in the way of prerequisites, other than being fit and having done a lot of relatively easy climbs, but Mick assured me casually, "It's just a matter of wanting to do it."

Even though I suffered prolonged and debilitating periods of doubt and fear during the first couple of days, Mick's indomitable and infectious willpower kept us going. Then in the middle of the third day, after a series of giant pendulum swings, we passed the point of no return, with all possibility of retreat cut off. Committed as we were, I remember that third bivouac as being the turning point in my life. Gone was all the stressful nagging fear and doubt, replaced by a profound sense of calm and peace. We took the time to look around and absorb the incredible drama and beauty of our situation. Empowered by this new-found confidence, we completed the rest of the climb without undue difficulty. After five days and four nights of unrelenting verticality, we staggered over the top onto flat ground and were greeted by a crowd of cheering fellow climbers who had hiked up the back, loaded with fresh fruit and beer, to help us celebrate the historic event.

I wrote an article about the climb, under the title of "Sorcerer's Apprentice," in which I attributed our success to psychic phenomena rather than conventional technical skill and expertise. A combination of Mick's ability to focus his will and positive intention, my allegiance and bonding to a fellow countryman a long way from home, the incredible generosity and support from the local climbers, the background aura of love and peace of the hippie movement at its peak and our awesome respect for El Cap and the beauty of Yosemite Valley all conspired to induce a remarkably high degree of synergy which dramatically enhanced our capabilities.

Proof that we had broken through the "aura of impossibility" that had previously kept El Cap in the domain of the gods was quickly supplied by the fact that right after our ascent all kinds of people started doing it.

"If those two bozos can do it so can we!" And they did: the four-minute mile phenomenon.

As the fall progressed and the rock climbing season in Yosemite wound down, along with a love affair with a California girl and my finances, some fellow Brits from Calgary invited me to join them in the basement of a favorite hangout for climbers in Calgary.

"It's a pretty rowdy scene. You'll fit right in!" they assured me.

Every weekend without fail the Rockies were invaded by crazy climbers from Calgary. As winter closed in, the rock climbing activities were curtailed, and while the bears were bedding in the backwoods, the beer in the bars of Banff continued to flow all the more. Paying for beer was one thing, but paying for outdoor recreation such as downhill skiing went against the grain of dedicated climbers, especially if there happened to be other fun to be had for free. As it turned out, there was an abundance of it: steep ice – virgin waterfalls – glistening in the pale winter sunshine right beside the highway, just asking, in this land of opportunity, to be seduced.

During my first winter in the Rockies, together with some of the other members of the Calgary Mountain Club (CMC), armed with new state-of-the-art ice climbing tools, in desperately cold but often sunny conditions, we pioneered the new sport of frozen waterfall climbing. We made first ascents of some of the more obvious falls that were close to roads, and then some of the longer, steeper and more remote ones were reconnoitred. Inevitably lessons were learned the hard way about survival in winter in the Canadian mountain wilderness, with its immense scale, its temperatures of thirty or forty below, its deep, dry powder snow and, of course, the dreaded avalanches. It was classic mountaineering adventure, exploring and pushing the internal and external limits. Clinging to these vertical pillars of glassy, hard, green ice with sharp ice picks and crampons like tigers' claws, way high up off the ground, was very primal and exhilarating but also extremely scary. Nobody knew for sure if it was possible to even *survive* such extreme conditions, never mind *succeed*.

One Sunday night four of us young climbers from Calgary sat around a bivouac camp on a precariously exposed ledge high up on a ridge, just below the summit of a big mountain. We had just completed a strenuous and scary ascent of its north face that had taken longer than expected and prevented us getting down off the mountain and returning to the city in time for work next morning. We were physically exhausted and had no food, but, far from feeling guilty, we relished the opportunity to savour and prolong the exhilarating sense of relief and release we were now feeling. The brilliant, sparkling stars and surrounding moonlit peaks accentuated our bliss. Our continuous stream of hysterical laughter pierced the profound silence of the deep mountain wilderness as we relived the more desperate moments on the climb.

"I was really gripped. Just about had brown britches a couple of times."

"It wasn't the fear that got me. It was the fear of fear!"

Gradually the peaceful environment calmed our emotions, and as we relaxed the conversation became deeper and more philosophical. We discussed how, after pushing the limits of hard climbing on the dangerous rock and ice faces of the Rockies, the price for fame, glory and ego satisfaction was getting higher and higher – especially when friends were being killed – and the rewards of questionable lasting value.

At the same time, I was noticing that the more time we spent in the pristine wilderness the greater was our enjoyment from simply being there, at peace with the magic of the landscape. The undiluted energy and pristine beauty inspired deep feelings of allegiance and love. Sometimes, as on this occasion, we became so engaged with the wild mountain environment that it seemed we had become part of it. As well as a heightened awareness and a shift of perception – no doubt inspired by adrenaline – that was conducive to increased performance and survival capability, we felt a deeply satisfying sense of connectivity with something larger than ourselves. This euphoric "natural high," which is now referred to as "being in the Zone," is what the three of us who were recent immigrants from Europe found so exciting and special about the Canadian wilderness experience.

When the subject of guilt about not showing up for work finally reared its ugly head, Bill, the one bona fide, laid-back Canadian, with his amiable sparkling eyes and his willing smile shining through a bushy beard and mop of dark curly hair, remarked, "There's nothing special about my job. I could probably easily get another one if I had to."

Bugs, the gaunt and wiry Scotsman, with typical, caustic humour added, "Going back to Calgary on Sunday nights, followed by Monday mornings, makes me puke."

Then the always positive and cheerful George, who grew up in the same Liverpool slum, with the same accent and exactly the same looks as George Harrison, and who had come to Canada to escape from work slavery in the factories of a big city, chipped in, "Wouldn't it be great to just stay out here in the mountains and not bother going back to Calgary? Maybe we should try it sometime."

I was not at all thrilled by my job at the City of Calgary Planning Department, which I considered a necessary evil to keep me close to the mountains, and was desperately looking for a way out. Sensing that Canada had much more to offer, my woolly-headed idealism seized the moment to ask, "Why don't we quit our jobs in the city and find ways to live permanently somewhere out in the wilds?"

As our minds gradually caught up with our weary bodies, but still sharing the heightened awareness of the pristine environment, we all agreed that weekends and holidays were no longer enough. A yearning we shared was to make being in the mountains part of our daily lives.

We made a pact.

And we made it happen.

Bill bought first a bow and arrow and then a kayak. With the first he took off into the Rockies. With the second he became Kayak Bill, spending the rest of his life travelling the BC coast, living completely off wild edible plants of the land and gathering wild food from the sea. George bought a 10-acre piece of raw land in the Columbia Valley near Golden and built himself a family homestead. Bugs moved out to the small town of Canmore in the Rockies.

Propelled by the still-undefined quest for freedom, I headed farther west until I reached the BC coast, where I found even more powerful satisfaction and romance to be waiting.

It may have taken a few years to detach ourselves incrementally from society's umbilical cord, but each of us, in our own way, succeeded in fulfilling the pact.

An interim step along the way was meeting Dick

Parsons, who lived most of the time in a tipi in a remote spot on the eastern slopes of the Rockies. He ran courses on survival and wild edible plants for the University of Alberta. Being far too proud and poor to pay to go on a course, a couple of us learned a lot from his lifestyle by hanging out at his tipi.

A few years of office work in Calgary had further exacerbated my disenchantment with the system to the point of being well primed for the encouragement the pact presented to opt out. Before I left Calgary I chanced to cross paths with a psychologist. Being pretty bigoted in those days I felt obliged to razz this guy about the importance of his vocation. His reply surprised and shook me a bit at the time, and much more later.

"Let's take you, for instance. What's your problem?"

"Me? I don't have a problem!" I assured him.

"Sure you do. What happened to you when you were about seventeen or eighteen?"

"Nothing much, played rugby, climbed, got ready to go to university."

"No, something really important."

That night I woke with a startling thought. "Oh yes! My mother died."

The psychologist smiled when I told him. He asked me a few questions about my mother and soon discovered that I could remember precious little about her. In fact I had never even thought of her once in the ten years since her death.

"That's your problem," he said. "When a teenage boy loses his mother he invariably develops a super-masculine persona to protect himself from the emotional trauma."

Searching a bit deeper, he discovered I had an older sister living in Vancouver. He recommended that I pay her a visit and talk with her about our mother. When I finally followed the free advice and showed up in Vancouver, my sister, Rachel, reminded me that mother was from a seafaring family. In fact, our grandfather had been an officer in the Royal Navy.

"That might explain why mother always took us to the seaside while dad always took us to the mountains," I realized, "and here I am arriving, at last, at a place that has an abundance of mountains and sea."

From then on, not only was I more open to psychology, I was much more open *period*, especially to all kinds of previously hidden connectivity in nature and life. I never looked back.

-3-
SETTLING DOWN

**"How and when did you find
a place to settle down?"**

IT DID NOT TAKE ME long after arriving on the BC
coast to realize that I had to have a boat. Boating,
especially sailing, would obviously be fun in itself
and would also provide access to the beautiful and
largely roadless mountains that could be seen on
every horizon, an explorer's paradise. My first boat
was a 21-foot sloop affectionately named *Shadowfax*

after Gandalf's horse that magically conveyed him to safety from the teeth of disaster in *Lord of the Rings*. Soon my old pal Bill showed up from the Rockies, and after a brief look at *Shadowfax* he suggested, with his usual mischievous grin, "Gee, that's great. Now we can sail up the coast and climb Mount Waddington."

"Good idea. Where is it, anyway?"

"Dunno. Must be up there somewhere."

We had heard Mount Waddington referred to as one of the world's great mountains, "a mountain-eer's mountain," which was the polite way of saying it was bloody difficult to climb. Whereas this casual attitude of ours may have been justified, as far as reaching the top of a mountain was concerned, we were about to find out it was sadly out of whack in terms of what was required to get even to the bottom of this one.

With only a smattering of marine savvy, learned in Sea Cadets at high school, and a few elementary preparations that included looking on a map, we cheerfully boarded *Shadowfax* and took off up coast on what seemed the most direct route to the mountain: up Bute Inlet and the

Homathko Valley, approximately 150 miles north of Vancouver.

During this exciting voyage the full range of hazards and difficulties that can be encountered by a small underpowered boat on this big, oh so big, coast was introduced to us the hard way. While storm-bound in a coastal pub we heard some old-timers arguing about the greatest coastal threat. Was it the tidal rapids with their 15-knot currents, three-foot overfalls and huge whirlpools? Or was it the southeaster with its hurricane force winds and mighty smoking waves turned chaotic by opposing tides? Or was it getting lost in the fog, going round and round in circles, running out of gas and freezing to death?

"Nah!" said one particularly crusty old fisherman, deliberately taking his time for maximum effect, "It's the rocks ... It's the effing rocks that get you."

So far we had managed to elude the "effing rocks," but on our recent adventures there had been some scary moments. Sailing north out of Powell River, up the open strait toward Desolation Sound, for instance, with a freshening southeaster on our stern quarter the boat would not stay on course and under our control. Even though we pulled the tiller as far as it would go to turn her downwind away from the increasingly alarming swells, she kept on wanting to swing back up to windward and into the waves. This, we later learned, was due to "weather helm," a safety feature built into every good sailboat causing the wind to spill out of the main sail and so reduce the risk of capsizing. Inadvertently, more by good feel than good judgment, we did the right thing, which was to reef, or reduce, the main sail. This elementary difficulty was typical of what is politely referred to as learning the hard way.

Another example of this learning style, which became our specialty, occurred when arriving after dark at one of the few-and-far-between anchorages. As *Shadowfax* nosed cautiously into the back of a large bay at the mouth of a large river, Bill was up on the bow making soundings to tell me how deep the water was.

Our desire to be close in against the shore for as much shelter as possible had to be balanced against the need of having enough water under our keel at low tide in the middle of the night. We figured that the ideal depth was 15 feet, but it needed to be that deep within the whole arc of swing of our anchor point. Just when it should have been about right, Bill yelled, "Five feet!" and before I had time to go in reverse he yelled, "Twenty feet!" This same pattern kept repeating, and eventually, having failed to make any rational sense of our measurements, we gave up in exhaustion and, hoping for the best, threw the anchor out and went to sleep. At low tide, early in the daylight hours, and after a luckily trouble-free night, the situation was explained: as the river flowed out through the tidal zone at the back of the bay it formed a "spit," or raised embankment, either side of its main channel. The mind boggles at the complex array of possibilities of what might have happened.

It turned out that Bute Inlet and Mount Waddington were too distant for such a slow, light boat and probably also too serious for her crew. But *Shadowfax* did make it to the head of Toba Inlet. The crew climbed a 9,000 ft. peak right out of the boat and were initiated, inevitably the hard way, into steep, rugged, trail-less terrain, impassably thick coastal bush, fiendishly prickly devil's club, horizontal-leaning slide alder and clouds of man-eating mosquitoes in otherwise idyllic, pristine alpine meadows.

From the Toba Inlet trip we learned to love the wild and rugged beauty of the Coast Range even more than the Rockies. It also became apparent that the greater availability of wild food, fish, oysters and clams, along with the relatively moderate climate, makes it much easier to survive off the land and sea on the coast than in the interior. We were also both inspired to start painting with watercolours. In synchronistic good fortune, that voyage also took us through Desolation Sound and the Discovery Island archipelago that later became my choice of place to settle down. I had noticed in passing at the time that it would be an interesting area to live in.

It was on the way back from this adventure that *Shadowfax* pulled into a derelict and characterful old dock in downtown Vancouver called Clay's Wharf. We'd heard it was the cheapest place to tie up. The first person we saw at the end of the dock was a beautiful, dark-haired hippie gal in a long, flowing dress, just standing there smiling and nursing a baby.

"Is it okay for us to tie up here?" we asked.

"Of course," she smiled. "Come on in."

The next thing we knew we were invited aboard a funky old boat and were drinking herb tea with a bunch of colourful, long-haired live-aboarders. It turned out that at least one of these shady-looking characters was one of the original members of Greenpeace, which had had its recent origins at that very same dock in downtown Vancouver. As the city had, not surprisingly, condemned the wharf to make way for their Granville Island redevelopment scheme, these folks were being evicted, and some of them were plotting to form a co-operative to buy a piece of land on a remote island up coast somewhere.

"In the spirit of flower power and brotherly love an' all that," the charismatic, persuasive and exceedingly hairy old hippie with rings in his nose and ears asked with a wry and sly chuckle, "how would you like to buy a share?"

Not being at all sure about the whole deal, for once in my short life I was cautious, and I used the honest excuse of not having enough money in order to postpone making any commitment. However, *Shadowfax* stayed tied up at the wharf during the last year or so before the eviction notices were finally posted, while I worked in the city to save up some money for a share in the land.

I had an opportunity to see the land before committing to buying the share in the co-op, which was just as well, since I had not yet convinced myself of the merits of gambling what to me was quite a bit of cash on such a shady-looking deal. A respectable job in Vancouver at the time enabled me to take out a loan, which was something I had never done before, and my rambler's heart did not relish the idea of being tied down to monthly payments. When I set foot on the island, however, all that doubt and uncertainty vanished in an instant. In fact, the hesitation had probably evaporated even before arriving at the island. Just the voyage up there from Powell River was an exhilarating adventure, especially the boat ride through the tidal rapids immediately prior to arrival at the destination.

A group of fellow enlistees in the co-op had quite sensibly organized a reconnaissance expedition and had invited me along. They chartered a sturdy old working sailboat, which turned out to be an excellent way to see the area and hear some tales and gossip of life beyond the end of the roads and power lines. The first part of the journey had been out in the open Georgia Strait, with enticing panoramic views of snow-capped mountains on both sides of the wide expanse of open sea. There was enough fresh breeze to set some sail, shut off the motor and feel the delightfully smooth rhythm of the classic old schooner heeling and heaving into the lively swell. Farther on we motored into the narrow channels that weave their way through the picturesque and heavily forested rocky shorelines of the cluster of islands squeezed between northern Vancouver Island and the remote mainland coast, at the top end of the Georgia Strait. This area has come to be known as the "Discovery Islands archipelago" after Captain Vancouver's famous ship, HMS *Discovery*.

The huge volume of water that enters and leaves the Georgia Strait basin twice daily, enough to vary the elevation as much as 15 feet on a big tide, has to find its way through these narrow channels four times a day, on its way in from and out to the ocean. As it squeezes though the narrowest channels, it accelerates to form some spectacular tidal rapids, some of which have 4-foot overfalls and whirlpools the size of tennis courts. We were lucky on this first occasion to be initiated into the vagaries of the rapids by an experienced, female old salt called Zoey at the helm of a very sturdy and experienced old boat called *Sailfish*, both of whom seemed to know exactly what they were doing. Although they took us through while the tide was still clipping along at an impressive rate, it was in the right direction, going with the flow and not against it. They also chose the line very carefully to avoid the worst of the whirlpools and turbulence.

"Beginners are advised to go through at slack water," Zoey explained.

"What's that?" asked one of the would-be islanders.

"The brief interval four times a day, when the flow of the rapids stops and changes direction," Zoey answered patiently, and then went on with a grin, "But we'll go through with the ebb running a bit. So hold on to your asses!"

Although the *Sailfish* rocked and rolled and accelerated to twice her previous speed, she and Zoey came through smiling, while we greenhorns gripped the handrails with white knuckles and collectively gasped, "Wow! What a rush!"

So by the time we pulled into the calm and serene little bay that was our destination, it's quite likely that I was already sold. Other than the occasional little beach shack there had been no sign of civilization for miles. As soon as the boat was tied up to the makeshift bundle of logs that served as a dock, the silence, beauty and peaceful serenity were a marvel. So too were the merganser ducks and blue herons in the back of the bay, the seals basking on the rocks and the eagle checking us out from his lookout on a branch, way up at the top of the magnificent old fir tree on the mossy bluffs nearby. This was exactly the kind of neighbourhood I was looking for.

A good hike around the property revealed a series of benches on south-facing slopes at the base of a dome-shaped mountain with fine views out to the ocean and neighbouring islands. Although it was hardly pristine, as it had been recently logged, the clear-cuts were relatively small and accessible by a network of skid roads.

"The clearings would likely make ideal spots for homesteads," one of the more practical visitors noticed, "and there was enough standing timber to use for building houses."

"Or to retain the integrity of the forest," another one argued, with shades of things to come.

The vibrations of the land itself felt good, inducing quite a lot of primal hooting and hollering from the woolly-headed visitors, including me, perhaps inspired by adrenaline. We built a camp and had a wonderful gathering around a huge fire with sleeping bags laid out under the stars, amid wind-twisted pine trees on an exposed mossy bluff overlooking the water. My imagination was working overtime on the fantasy of building a home and settling down in such a beautiful and stimulating place.

Next morning the sadness at having to leave the island and go back to the city one more time was outweighed by the exhilaration of knowing the decision to buy into the land co-op deal had been made.

"How did you two meet?," a female apprentice asked Laurie eagerly. "Was it love at first sight?"

WHILE ROB WAS LIVING ON *Shadowfax* at Clay's Wharf and working in the city to pay off the loans on his boat and the land, one night in the climber's pub in Vancouver, he complained to the old patron of the west coast climbing community, Jim Sinclair, that he wasn't having much luck with the local ladies.

"I know just the girl for you," Jim responded. "Her name is Laurie Manson. She's going to be in Squamish this weekend."

So, he set us up for a blind date in "The Chieftain," a climbers' bar in Squamish. Without telling Rob, Jim had phoned me and asked if I wanted to meet a famous ice climber from the Rockies.

"He has long, scruffy, blond hair and will be wearing a red windbreaker.... By the way, he's a bit of a lad, so you'd better watch out," Jim had warned me.

I had been brought up in Squamish and had learned to climb with a group of local climbing desperadoes who called themselves "The Squamish Hard Core." They trained on the fierce walls of the local granite massive known as "The Chief." They were some of the world's best rock climbers but they had a wild and lawless lifestyle. Partly under their influence, at the age of 20, together with some other girlfriends I had become a good enough climber to make some first all-female ascents, including "The Grand Wall" on The Chief and the "Diamond" face of Long's Peak in Colorado, and was just then developing it into a career as an instructor.

Being used to the Squamish Hard Core, I was not at all intimidated by the climbers' usual disorderly barroom behaviour, and I was not surprised to find Rob and his buddies already quite drunk at seven in the evening. First impression aside, I knew he was a famous ice climber, so he must have had something going for him. I suppose by the end of that week end I was attracted by Rob's energy, his ideas and his sincerity. It might have been bullshit but at least it was heartfelt.

"How about you, Rob, was it love at first sight for you?" Everyone in the steamed-up cabin laughed.

I WAS PROBABLY TOO DRUNK to notice at the time, but I remember thinking next day when I saw Laurie climbing that any girl who could climb that well could do pretty well anything she put her mind to. I was right about that at least. We hit it off right away and arranged to meet again at the Outdoor Centre where Laurie was working in the Vancouver Island mountains and living with her four-year-old daughter, Kiersten. I was immediately impressed by the quiet strength and inner peace that both Laurie and Kiersten possessed and by the delightful, natural intimacy of their relationship. This was exactly the kind of sincere integrity that I was escaping to, and the lack of which, in society, I was escaping from.

The attraction served to pull me away from the city, farther out into the wild, rugged and remote coastal landscape where the powerful combination of mountains, forests and ocean calmed my restless spirit and inspired me to take the plunge. Finally, I turned my back on the city and professional life and the security of steady income, for good. I bought the share in the land co-op and invited Laurie and Kiersten to join me in "the back to the land movement," carving out a living from scratch, on a remote and beautiful west coast island.

"So it was love at first sight, then?"

YES. INDEED IT WAS.

"That's about it for one night," I announced wearily and we all turned in.

Next morning the storm continued and so did the stories.

-4-
COSMIC SHACK

"How did you get started living on raw land?"

WE FINALLY ARRIVED ON THE island for good on board *Shadowfax* late in the fall of '75. Having finally paid off the loans on the boat and the land and quit my job in the city, I had sailed up from Vancouver and lured Laurie and Kiersten away from the relative security of the Outdoor Centre. It was the end of their season and Laurie was being laid off, anyway. It was late in the day when we tied up at the makeshift dock, so we made ourselves comfortable in *Shadowfax*'s tiny cabin, which would become our home for the next few weeks until we found a place to build some kind of shelter on the land. The other families were already ensconced in tiny plywood cabins, each with its own clearing in the forest, a few minutes' walk up the hill from the dock.

Choice of family house site location was on a very informal first come, first served basis, and we were last on the list. Although the most obvious house sites had already been taken, a magnificent spot among a pocket of old growth trees overlooking the ocean on the edge of two acres of logging slash remained unclaimed.

With hardly any tools, no practical skills and very little in the way of money or equipment, we built a tent platform that quickly evolved into a primitive shack, using fir poles for a frame enclosed with cedar shake walls and roofs, all taken right out of the forest. We used plastic poly for windows and egg cartons stapled on the walls for insulation. The shack was very drafty, especially when the southeasters blew. You could see daylight through the roof and walls but it didn't leak. For us, after living for a few weeks in a small, damp and crowded boat, in true Monty Python's Four Yorkshiremen tradition, it was "sheer luxury."

Though constantly being upgraded, but with the total cost not amounting to more than a thousand dollars, it housed our family and pets for 12 years. I'm ashamed to admit now, however, that the reason tall people had to duck to avoid bumping their heads on the low ceiling in the kitchen was that I had measured the height by using multiples of a six-inch nail and failed to realize that six-inch nails in Canada are only five and a half inches. I discovered this during a visit from Laurie's brother, Steve, who, having evidently noticed our stone-age equipment and exceedingly crude carpentry, gave us a Christmas present of a tape measure, a square and a level. Too polite to offer to show us how to use them, in a masterful understatement he said:

"You could probably use these."

Water supply was initially buckets filled from nearby running streams. When these streams dried up in the summer and froze up in winter, water had to be imported by boat from larger but distant streams. Some elementary water divining led us to dig a crude well in the forest up the mountain. This, more by good luck than good research, turned out to be a real well. In addition to collecting surface water as a reservoir, it had fresh groundwater seeping into it. A great deal of trial and error determined a way of siphoning the deliciously fresh water up out of the well and gravity-feeding it down the hill through 18 hundred-foot lengths of one-inch plastic pipe to our cabin.

Our first real luxury, running water, into the kitchen sink!

Heat was from hand-split firewood burning in a stove made from a recycled 45-gallon steel oil drum onto which a friend on the next island had welded a steel door and a six-inch stovepipe chimney. One of the great surprises for me was that as well as the immediate community of a dozen or so neighbours in the land co-op, most of whom were as green as us, there were, scattered around the neighbouring islands, a few very resourceful and practical craftsmen. The same guy who helped build the stove also improvised a cunning coil of copper pipe around the stovepipe that gave us a very simple but effective hot water system.

Bingo again. We had hot water galore. Super sheer luxury!

A minute's walk out in the clearing, which eventually became a meadow, was the outhouse, a hole in the ground covered by a tiny, three-walled hut. The open side faced strategically away from the general traffic pattern. The throne was a carefully dimensioned hole cut into the plywood bench with a plastic toilet seat tacked in place around it. The seat itself was soon upgraded to a doughnut of cushy Styrofoam, after a visit from my older sister Catherine, who was inclined to compare the relative merits of the loos of the world – she had written a guide book on the topic. She announced in her most flamboyant manner:

"I don't mind roughing it a bit, but a bare bum on a frigid plastic seat first thing in the morning is a bit too much!"

From the perspective of today's green technology, the old-fashioned outhouse scores highly and is a relatively healthy, low impact, carbon neutral and waterless way to dispose of human waste. More important, perhaps, to us was the daily, bracing ritual that offered a meditative and uplifting, spiritual experience. While not exactly smelling of roses, the quiet privacy, unobstructed view and exposure to the elements provided an opportunity to listen to the birds sing, the wind howl or the rain spatter against the roof – generally, to absorb the ambience of the land while reflecting on the true nature of the universe.

Lighting through the long winter evenings was from candles and old-fashioned kerosene lamps, which, though romantic for a while, were soon found to be dangerous, polluting and difficult to keep clean. The most prestigious model was the famous Aladdin, which, although it gave a superior light when working properly, turned out to be notoriously finicky to keep clean, while the slightest draft made the delicate mantles flare up and burn out. Fortunately for us, we had a visit in the early days from a friend in Vancouver who was a physics prof at UBC doing research on solar panels. After seeing our oil lamps he insisted on giving us a used solar panel and showing us how to hook it up to a car battery.

Bingo again! We had the extreme "sheer luxury" of power to the people in the shape of one fluorescent light bulb in our makeshift kitchen. This was a great status symbol and was the envy of the neighbourhood. Now, with our one electric light, we were considered to be really "upwardly mobile."

Another mod con that was also powered by the solar panel and car battery was a marine VHF radio that boat people and remote logging camps used for making phone calls through the Campbell River marine operator. These devices were designed to be on boats, but most folks living on remote islands had them in their houses. Each station had a name and number which was usually the name of a boat, and every transmission started by calling up the Campbell River operator. For example, we would press the transmit button and speak into the microphone, "*Shadowfax* calling Campbell River radio." When the operator answered we would ask to be connected to our required phone number.

The interesting part and, for us cabin-fevered country bumpkins, the entertaining one, was that because there was no privacy on the call, everyone on the whole coast could hear the conversation.

This was particularly hilarious when one of the parties, usually the one making the call, was familiar with the system and would very often be cagey about what they said while the other person would not hesitate to divulge all kinds of sensitive, often intimate and personal information. Later the system was improved to provide privacy, but only for the party making the call. So the audience was provided with an extra layer of entertainment, elevating it in value to the status of mystery drama, having to guess, deduce or imagine what the person was saying when only hearing the bleep, bleep, bleeps.

For instance a typical call my go like this:

"Say, Honey, when you comin' home?"

"Bleep, bleep, bleep"

"Can you send me some money?"

"Bleep."

I also remember being entertained for hours by the Shakespearean tragicomedy that was being played out every night in our living room between the cat and the dog. Laurie and Kiersten would have to translate the subtle body language to clue me in to what the animals were really thinking. For instance, the cat would be trying to let us know it was suppertime, but rather than lose face and have to lower her dignity by demanding attention herself, she would bug the dog and get her to bark and rattle her doggy dinner bowl instead.

Laurie embarked on what would gradually become a lifetime vocation, a fine organic garden inside a stockade fence of cedar pickets to keep the deer out. The garden was (and still is) her pride and joy. She also kept chickens and sometimes geese and ducks. We were given a couple of geese for a wedding present two years after arriving on the land. We called them Pierre and Margaret after Prime Minister Trudeau and his wife.

I did a lot of the grunt work in the garden while Laurie did the cultivating. We bought seeds, started them in the greenhouse and prepared the soil with compost made from household scraps, chicken manure and seaweed. We brought in pigs to help break up and fertilize the land. We used an old gas-fired rototiller to plow the ground, and we planted in May when the soil warmed up. Summertime brought abundant harvests and the vegetables tasted delicious. Many, such as root crops, Brussels sprouts, leeks and kale, stayed in the ground and we used them all through the winter. Although greatly expanded and somewhat more sophisticated now, the original organic garden is still the mainstay of our homestead lifestyle many years later.

Although I was initially in my life deprived of any but the most elementary experience with using tools, my academic training had fostered a keen interest in vernacular architecture. Dwellings made from local materials that blend into their surroundings with elegant simplicity invariably possess a timeless quality that expresses unique, personal joy and pride in the instinctive process of human nest building.

"Wouldn't it be wonderful," I had often vaguely imagined, "to witness that kind of authentic form of self-expression?"

Fantasy alone could not possibly have replicated the depth of pleasure the actual experience would turn out to be. It's almost as if all my previous adventures had been preparing me for this. What an incredible bonus the Canadian wilderness offers for those brave enough to commit to living beyond the grid! It allows the absolute freedom to manifest this basic human impulse unfettered by all the conventional codes and standards intended to protect us from making our own mistakes. It was especially satisfying to share that elemental experience with two young ladies I loved.

Again with apologies to Monty Python, what is unquestionably true is that in spite of "'aving it tuff in them days, we were very 'appy," in our old cosmic shack.

"And if you're trying to tell that to us young people today, we won't believe a word of it!" interjected one young skier.

5

BACK TO THE LAND COMMUNITY

"Was the community a hippie commune?"

WE DIDN'T EXACTLY THINK OF it as such at the time but it probably amounted to that in the end. The original founding intention was to beat the capitalistic system by collectively purchasing a large piece of land at a relatively low cost per acre and sharing it without subdivision, rather than separately buying many smaller, more expensive pieces. Most of the members attempted to follow the traditions of self-sufficiency and self-reliance of the Canadian pioneers and share the goals and aspirations of the hippie movement: peace, love and communal living. There was also a looser common goal of incorporating the spirit of adventure and direct involvement with nature into our daily lives and sharing it with our kids.

There were ten families in the land co-operative, and we had bought the quarter section (160 acres) of south-facing waterfront property from a logging company that had just finished logging the land for the second time. Fortunately, it had not all been clear-cut, and although there were fresh-cut patches there were also areas of standing timber between them. The island had no paved roads, water supply, electricity or telephones. The nearest connection with the public road access was a remote dirt road several miles away on the next island. There were, however, some old logging skid roads on the property, and the co-op had purchased a second-hand tractor. We brought it in on a barge, and it worked surprisingly well for transporting loads up from the makeshift dock up to the house sites.

Initially, most of our time was spent clearing house sites in the patches of logging slash. This work was done by hand except for chainsaws, the tractor and a few primitive tools. We would buck up all the old logging slash and debris with a chainsaw, drag the pieces with the tractor, then manhandle them onto huge burn piles. We scored dynamite from our logging friends and used it to blow up the old stumps. Even though clearing land by hand in this way was commonly referred to as back-breaking work, it was very satisfying. Working the land, you don't need a plan. You just go out in the morning and start dealing with what is most obviously in need of attention. Then one thing leads on to the next. At the end of the day you're tired but satisfied by the visible progress; you're energized by the combination of vigorous exercise, fresh air and the energy of the land itself. We often worked collectively on each other's places and developed good camaraderie (most of the time), with lots of potluck suppers and sharing of child care duties. Because there were no cars, everywhere we went on the land was on foot and by boat on the ocean, so we were all in pretty good shape.

"How did you get by without regular jobs?"

THE RELATIVELY LOW COST OF living was considerably augmented by voluntarily reduced material standards, particularly of housing and domestic services. Most people lived in home-built shacks, as we did, heated by simple thin metal wood stoves that acquired the affectionate self-deprecating label of "hippie stoves," very primitive if any plumbing, no electricity and no cars or insurance. We grew some vegetables right away, but it took many years to build up the soil to get any serious production from gardens. We gathered valuable wild edible food such as stinging nettles in the spring and chanterelle mushrooms in the fall. There were so many fish close by that we could easily catch enough for supper just by dropping a line and jigging for cod or red snapper. In the summertime the local guys had competitions called derbies to see who could catch the biggest salmon. Thirty-pounders were very common. Some of those same guys would hunt deer in the fall. So there was always a lot of smoked salmon or venison as well as clams, oysters and prawns being offered and or traded around the neighbourhood. Some folks would take seasonal work such as tree planting, logging, fishing and wilderness guiding, which, though it took them away from home, often meant going farther out into the wilds with even more uncertainty and adventure.

All of these traditional, part-time ways of making a living on remote parts of the coast had in common not only a deep respect for the elements but also a positive attitude toward adversity and a willingness to commit to the flow of events. Just like mountaineering, surviving without getting hurt required a high degree of self-reliance and full responsibility and accountability for the consequences of one's own actions. It also generated profoundly satisfying communion both with nature and with each other that could and did become addictive.

"We've heard that hippies liked to dance and have orgies. Was there any of that in your island community?"

WE CELEBRATED JUST ABOUT EVERY pagan occasion possible with wild and outrageous parties and dances that often lasted for days. All the problems associated with "making a living" or "getting things done" faded into the background, replaced by camaraderie, live music, dancing galore, communal feasting, good vibrations and fun.

Winter Solstice was always particularly important because it meant the sun was coming back and the long winter evenings would be getting shorter again. Saluting the sun made a lot of sense when the lack of light during the winter months was more psychologically challenging than bad weather. At solstice we made up for it with dancing and singing around huge bonfires.

Mardi Gras was always a colourful and hilarious event because we had one couple from New Orleans who were serious party animals and insisted on teaching "y'all" how to let it "all hang loose." They made us up, especially the kids, with elaborate, homemade, fancy costumes, masks and face paint. They wandered around with big sorcerer's staffs with ribbons and bells on them, shouting, "Happen everybody! ... Happen!"

Blossom parties were delightful celebrations of the arrival of spring. Summer Solstice was usurped by our co-op's particular specialty, Leo Parties.

Astrology was quite popular, and August is the time of year of the fire sign, Leo. We had several co-op members with birthdays in Leo, and Leos being fiery types they made sure everybody else had to share their celebration of themselves.

Hundreds of hippies descended on our property, camping out and partying for three days on these occasions every summer. We would set up a Mexican street stand-type restaurant under a pole shack and tarp and take turns at churning out burritos and gallons of homebrewed beer. We also put on pantomimes with a different theme every year, with fancy dress and the whole works. All the co-op adults and kids were involved.

In the most memorable Leo party of all, the theme for the pantomime was Star Wars and the show was due to start right after lunch. It had been blowing southeast and raining all morning, but then right on cue, with great karmic synchronicity, the wind switched to westerly (good weather wind) and the sun came out. The kids especially were very excited about getting the show started. Trouble was, within minutes the westerly wind was blowing a gale. Some of us were really alarmed when we saw trees starting to come down all around where the kids and visitors had congregated. We considered postponing the show and trying to direct people to shelter until we realized that there was no way anything on these occasions could be directed or managed. These events had a life of their own. The whole thing was essentially anarchic and karmic. Plus on our forested property there was nowhere else to go that was more sheltered or safe. We were in nature's hands.

The show went on and the wind increased to storm force. Just as Darth Vader made his dramatic appearance walking slowly down the main road, a huge alder crashed down just yards behind him and then another in front of him. Of course the audience cheered wildly and the kids screamed hysterically. It was the ultimate in theatrical drama. Hemlock trees were snapping in the middle, with the top halves of the trees flying through the air and crashing down in the bush hundreds of feet away. The "Force" must have been with us because, miraculously, no one was hurt and the show was the success of a lifetime.

"What was it that was most different about the alternative lifestyle?"

ONE OF THE MOST REMARKABLE novelties (that still continues to surprise visitors) was the depth of the prevailing silence. An awe-inspiring sensation in itself, this peaceful background influence had a profoundly calming effect on the mind and also accentuated the orchestration of sounds and other sensory stimulation when they did occur. Bird calls, for instance, such as woodpeckers hammering, ravens croaking, eagles squeaking, robins whistling, pierced the silence of the forest with a sharp clarity of tone and frequency that never failed to catch our attention. The sad cries of gulls and terns rang out across the channel and right into our hearts as great flocks circled and dove for fish in the rapids. With even the gentlest of breezes, tree branches swayed and danced, while ripples and wavelets broke up the reflections of sunlight on the water into oval-shaped pools of colour, catching our notice and reminding us of west coast Native art.

As tidal currents swirled the ocean, the light in the sky, though often limited to varying shades of grey in bad weather, moved both external and my personal wave reflections, in a dynamic and moody dance. Emanating from the silence, the powerful ambient energy of the land, the sea and the elements was not merely auditory or aesthetic; it spoke directly to our emotions, reawakening my childhood feelings of allegiance for the mysterious hidden connectivity. It reminded me of "the pact" and the essential motivation for embarking on this adventurous experiment in living on the edge of wilderness.

Like many other young people at that time, we explored the excitement and intrigue of alternative forms of consciousness. Perception and awareness of the vibrating energy fields of the environment was heightened by the ingestion of mild psychotropic plants such as psilocybin mushrooms and marijuana, which were relatively harmless, cheap and readily available. It was quite a common sight on the BC west coast in those days to see colourful long-haired hippies on their hands and knees in local farmers' fields looking for magic mushrooms or carrying buckets of water to pot gardens hidden in the woods.

When I tried mushrooms it was initially quite scary. I was giggling and babbling so uncontrollably I could no longer communicate and had to slip away into the woods on my own. I found a mossy glade with sunlight shafting through the forest and a pretty view out to the ocean. Here I stripped off my clothes, lay down on my back in the warm moss and relaxed. As I gazed up into the amazingly complex, intricate and dazzling web of branches that formed the forest canopy, all normal sense of being a separate individual entity with a name, an identity and the ability to control my circumstances, dissolved into a continuous, pulsating flow of energy. There was no separation of internal and external, this or that. Far from being threatening and fearsome, this new sensation was conducive to entering a timeless, thoughtless and pleasing pulse of awareness, with an increasingly reassuring realization that the trees, rocks, flowers and mountains were all similarly, harmoniously pulsating. In this way the initial fear was gradually replaced by an enticing and euphoric feeling of being part of the interflow of energy linking all things, including me, in a single continuous process. At that point I got up on my feet and slowly walked around, overwhelmed by a flood of joy and happiness. I do believe I even hugged a few trees and chatted with some chickadees that were chirping around. I gazed in infinite, timeless wonder at the close-up beauty and intricacy of the wings of a butterfly that landed on my naked belly, tears rolling down my cheeks.

"Couldn't you do this without drugs?"

YES, TO A DEGREE, AND it didn't take me long to realize the drugs were unnecessary. Although this takes conscious effort, imagination and discipline, previous experience helps. The drugs assist in "rattling one's cage," breaking through the conditioned mental constructs of the subconscious mind that govern a very high percentage of our thoughts, actions and emotions in modern society. It is particularly difficult, especially for men, it seems, to let go of their egos, which get in the way of the truth by insisting on fitting everything into preconceived boxes so they can be controlled and manipulated. The opposite effect of opening our minds, being more fully in the moment, more conscious, more alive, can be achieved in varying degrees through meditation or yoga, in fact from any deep-breathing physical exertion in fresh air, especially when accompanied by the fear-induced "rush" of the "natural high" with which I was already so familiar.

"Just like riding a big wave or carving a perfect turn in the deep powder, you mean?"

EXACTLY. WE BECOME ONE WITH the wave or the mountain and they tell our body/minds how to perform.

"Like being in the Zone, you mean?" a young skier chipped in with engaged enthusiasm.

YES, PRECISELY.

Ultimately it was the experience of spending so much time directly engaged with the energy fields of the wild natural environment on the island that awakened our minds and bodies to previously hidden connectivity and synchronicities of the life all around and within us. It was the shared sensation of oneness with the "good vibrations" of the land that we cherished so much that instilled a sense of community and substantiated our faith in love and peace.

This is why it is so important to preserve our remaining wilderness. It tells us how to survive and prosper if we can but open our body/minds to hearing and feeling its message.

"What happened to the back to the land community?"

UNFORTUNATELY, IT ALSO HAS TO be said that, being in the moment, conscious and in tune with the environment are much easier said than done, especially over a long period of time. When, for any of an infinite numbers of reasons, we succumb to the powerful myths of fear and separation, remain trapped in our subconscious control dramas and fail to be in tune with our surroundings, bad things such as accidents, illnesses, arguments and even wars are more likely to happen. Our back to the land community suffered its fair share of these challenges to sustainable cohesion and synergy.

Even though we managed to stay true to the basic agreement of sharing the enjoyment of the land and love for all the children, like other alternative communities of the period we were to find out the hard way, as T.S. Eliot said, that "between the idea and the reality ... falls the shadow." The practicality of sharing tools and equipment wore thin, and huge personality conflicts severely tested our idealistic expectations of each other and communal living in general. We all abhorred formality and bureaucracy, but it turned out that the strongest advocates of informality were in practice habitual dictators. If things were not to be done their way they would exercise a veto and prevent them being done at all. The result was that any attempts to function collectively or even democratically were miserable failures. Eventually we all learned that the best way to get along was by backing off on lofty communal projects and expectations, leaving each other alone and doing our own thing.

Some of us, who were closer friends than others, found mutually agreeable arrangements for co-operating. Certainly the children bene- fited tremendously from their happy experiences of growing up in such an adventurous physical environment and acquiring deeply ingrained self-confidence and self-reliance. They also ben- efited from their tribal experience of belonging to an extended family, acquiring a deep bond and love for each other. In spite of the incessant, unglamorous squabbling among the adults, we succeeded in protecting the kids from the brunt of the negativity and fulfilled, temporarily at least, the primary goal of creating an alternative community in spite of ourselves.

6

ISLAND SCHOOLING

"What about the kids? Were they high too?"

NOT ON DRUGS. THEY WERE naturally high, engaging with the magic of the landscape and with each other. Kiersten and six other young co-op children close to her age lived together as an extended family, sleeping with different parents every night in whichever household they ended up in. Most of their time was spent playing barefoot in the forest and on the beaches. You could say they were "free range" kids. Even though we knew there were cougars around, the parents never worried about the kids and sometimes didn't know exactly where they were. Parents were heard to say things like "Has any one seen the kids lately? I haven't seen them for days."

This is not as irresponsible as it might sound, because part of the reward of coming to terms with all the variables of living on the remote coast, especially in a tribal situation, was that through experience we learned to trust a sixth sense that provided access to a collective heightened awareness of our surroundings. Between all of us parents, someone would in fact know pretty well where the kids were and what they were doing. We had also noticed how prevalent this deeper, intuitive and instinctive consciousness, knowing without knowing, was among the old-timers we had met, especially fishermen, tugboatmen and loggers who spent a lot of time doing very dangerous work out in the wilds and had developed uncanny survival instincts. It was another example of being in the Zone.

This is exactly the kind of wisdom I had glimpsed

while climbing in the Rockies, and also something that appealed to hippie sensibilities because it was a manifestation of the way loving consciousness can be used to overcome fear of the unknown. It supported and substantiated the demand for peace by showing that violence was not the only or even the most effective way of responding to dangerous external threats.

Perhaps even more important was the way this attitude influenced the kids themselves, so that they were not afraid. Our belief, supported by experience and traditional example, was that the behaviour of the animals was affected by our demeanour and intentions, and vice versa. If we thought and behaved like victims the vibrations of our body language would make wild animals more inclined to interpret us as victims. Conversely, if we were not threatened by their presence they would be less likely to be threatened by ours.

Co-op kids were taken three days a week in small boats in all kinds of weather for two miles through the tidal rapids to the one-room elementary school a couple of miles away on the adjacent island. The school had been closed for many years until a small group of us local parents succeeded in persuading the local school board to reopen it even though there were only about ten kids who would attend on a regular basis.

Because of the difficulty of negotiating rapids on a twice-daily basis in small boats with old outboard motors, we bought an old floathouse that had been a logging camp cookhouse. We tied it up at the government dock just down the hill from the school and fitted some bunks and used it as a hostel for the kids to stay in overnight. We also managed to talk the school board into a three-day school week, and the parents took turns house parenting the kids for the two nights at the floathouse.

This was the era of the Trudeau government's Local Initiatives Program (LIP), and one of our parents who had been a lawyer (the original Greenpeacer who had started our co-op) knew how to file grant applications. We applied for funding to upgrade the kids' accommodation from the (even by our primitive standards) rather slummy floathouse at the dock to a brand new timber frame bunkhouse at the school site. Part of the small print of the grant application required that the project satisfy all local planning and health requirements. The school board administration, which had originally been hostile to our endeavours to help ourselves, had quite surprisingly softened up because by some mysterious fluke our children had remarkably good academic records.

No such luck, however, with the local health inspector, who was not at all sympathetic to the traditional outhouses we were proposing to use for toilets. We had a meeting inside the old float-house with six of the interested parties, three on each side of the tiny kids' table squeezed tightly between the bunks. On one side of the negotiating table were three of us local dads. On the other side were the federal government bureaucrat, who thankfully was on our side, the rather posh ex-British army secretary treasurer of Campbell River School Board and, wedged tightly in between them, the hugely obese and hairy-bellied Campbell River health inspector.

The climax of the meeting occurred when the health inspector finally made it clear that he stubbornly refused to budge an inch from his original position of demanding proper flush toilets with a hugely expensive septic treatment plant. At this point, to our absolute amazement, the secretary treasurer said in his most pompous English military accent: "The Federal Government of Canada seems prepared to put a blind eye to the telescope. The School Board of Campbell River is prepared to do the same. I don't see why the Health Authority shouldn't do so too."

In the end we got round the health inspector, in spite of his massive girth, by successfully applying for funding to build, not a "dormitory," but a rather fine "storage shed" to store our children in while they attended school.

Speaking of outhouses, there was another incident that went down in the "bunkhouse hall of fame" and illustrates how different were the values of what we considered politically correct parenting in those days. Generally we parents were permissive when it came to controlling our kids' behaviour, but part of the self-reliance code was accountability and acceptance of responsibility for the consequences of one's actions. When it was time to draw a line in the dirt, remedial measures were often swift and decisive, though rarely violent or unjust.

There was one particularly mischievous and outright naughty big kid who tended to bully the smaller ones in the school playground. He was accused of having deliberately thrown a younger kid's soccer ball down the outhouse hole. When his dad heard about it, he took the culprit by the legs and dangled him head first down the outhouse hole to retrieve the soccer ball.

In spite of horrendous logistical problems and personality conflicts among the parents, the kids enjoyed the experiment in communal living, and even now those who attended the bunkhouse have strong and long-lasting friendships and happy memories, another extended family, essentially.

Not so the parents. The basic idea was that the parents should send as much food to the bunk-house each week as the kids would eat at home. Unfortunately, there was one family who had three kids and used the opportunity not to bother sending much if any food. I listened to all kinds of whining by the other parents. When it was my turn to host, the three kids showed up for three days with three loaves of bread. At the end of the shift I sent a note back home with the kids for the parents saying, "Even Jesus needed some fishes."

This did not go down well with those parents, and I heard through the grapevine that they said they were going to kill me.

Soon after the new bunkhouse was completed, the school board introduced a travel allowance which enabled the parents to buy newer outboard motors and run the kids to school and back home each day, so the bunkhouse sleepover days were finished.

At that point the very fine timber frame building served first as a classroom and later, when the school board built new classrooms, as a community meeting room. It has continued to do so ever since. Over the years the pride people have in the characterful and charming timber frame building has contributed to a very strong symbiotic relationship between the outer islands community and the school. Both are benefiting from and dependent on each other in what could be considered as a genuinely effective and successful community school.

-7-
DOMESTIC ANIMALS

"Did you have any animals?"

OF COURSE.

When Kiersten was eleven, she just had to have a horse. It turned out to be her soulmate, a wonderful character named Riskie, part quarterhorse, part Morgan, a brown mare with a cute white stripe on her forehead. I was impressed by and jealous of the obvious rapport the two of them enjoyed.

Kiersten was amused by my lack of comfort

around the horse. For a start, Riskie was quite big and very powerful and definitely had a mind of her own. She was what horse people call "spirited." I called her "Frisky Riskie." Laurie and Kiersten pointed out that I had a bad attitude and my nervousness made Riskie more aggressive toward me.

It took me quite a while to get over this problem. They recommended I should feed her and give her treats as well as stroking and petting her more often. Particularly impressive was her ability to find her way back home after long outings into the interior of the island. Once I discovered that she could do some work my attitude changed a bit. I built a wooden pannier that sat on top of her saddle and could be filled with various loads such as boxes of groceries and firewood. In the fall we would travel several miles to an old homestead to load her up with apples. I was truly awed by the weight she would happily carry over rough ground. She could carry ten of my armloads of firewood. The only proviso was that four o'clock sharp was quitting time and she headed for the barn.

Eventually I did overcome my hang-up and Riskie allowed me to work with her, but much to

Kiersten's hilarity, I failed miserably in my one and only attempt to ride her.

Riskie's greatest claim to fame was the time she boarded our catamaran, *Quintano*, and sailed into Heriot Bay. I had assumed this was a joke when Laurie and Kiersten first suggested it, and when I saw them lead her down the ramp and onto our dock I still could not believe they were serious. I walked away shaking my head, refusing to have anything to do with it. To my absolute amazement Kiersten calmly walked Riskie down the ramp, along the dock, up the makeshift plywood ramp, over the combing and down into *Quintano's* cockpit. No problem at all.

Kiersten tied her halter to the mast step inside the cabin and off we went through the rapids. We even had a favourable enough breeze to put up the jib and sail for a while. There were some quite big waves, and as the boat rocked gently from side to side, Riskie swayed her bum to help keep her balance. Her head was up and her ears pricked, which showed she was enjoying herself. As the boat came into Heriot Bay we raised a few eyebrows. By the time Riskie walked up the ramp at the public dock a crowd had gathered and they all cheered when she stepped off the top of the ramp onto the landing. Kiersten jumped on her back and trotted off down the road. I was left to clean up the poop she had deposited on one of *Quintano*'s winches (henceforth known as the "poop deck").

During the first ten years on the land we had a female tortoiseshell cat called Tweedy who had a lot of kittens. At first I was in the habit of drowning some of them, which did not go down well with the kids, so I thought I'd be clever and use the opportunity of throwing a gunny sack full of rocks and kittens into the sea to give the kids a lecture in elementary biology. I was explaining why we had to control the cat population. When asked where the kittens came from, I was attempting to tiptoe around the honest answer only to find the kids giggling hilariously at my prevarications. What finally stopped me dead in my tracks was when one of the youngest little girls blurted out with great glee, "Yeah. And that's what all of that humping is all about."

So much for politically correct child rearing.

From then on 8-year-old Kiersten took charge

of the situation and insisted on giving the kittens away when she went to town. I thought it would take forever to stand outside the supermarket and dispose of four kittens. Not so. Kiersten had them all gone in an hour. What's more, she continued to do so for many years after. She became known by a whole generation of Campbell River folks as "the kitten girl."

When we finally decided to have Tweedy spayed, our vet friend Marlene generously offered to visit the school and give an educational spaying and neutering class. She invited all the local kids from the surrounding islands to bring their cats to school for the occasion. Everything went well with the females, including Tweedy, but when Marlene performed the surgery on the first male kitten several of the young boys in the class fainted.

More recently we had another female, black and white cat called Irish. She acquired her name because she had such a wild and rebellious spirit. Her previous owner had kept her, her mom and her siblings underneath their house rather than inside it. They gave her to us after the rest of her family had been taken out by a cougar. She responded well to our hospitality and Laurie's animal witchery and became extremely domesticated and affectionate. She offered me a daily lesson in the giving of unconditional love. When my attention strayed out of the here and now, which it invariably did quite quickly, like a Zen master with his stick she put out a demanding paw and if the deviance was not remedied right away there was just enough exceedingly sharp claw action to ensure a speedy remediation. I never ceased to be amazed at how comfortably she could nestle into the contours of my lap and how grounded that made me feel. In spite of her wildness, Irish didn't bother going out at all when it was really cold or wet. On the contrary it was impressive how close she could get to the wood stove without being cooked, how deep inside our bedcovers she could snuggle and how much of the time she could sleep.

The cat we have now showed up at a community meeting. A neighbour from the next island had a cardboard box sitting on the table, and when the meeting got boring someone asked, "What's in the box?" Without answering, he lifted the lid and four tiny grey and white kittens jumped out.

One of them, quick as a flash, ran across the table, bounced off my lap, up onto my shoulder and calmly sat there and looked at everybody. "Rob. You've been chosen. It's your cat now!" For the first time at the meeting everyone agreed. I seconded the motion.

Smokey has turned out to be a very pretty cat with all the qualities of Tweedy and Irish and more so. A wicked mouser, she is wild and independent at the same time, extremely affectionate, sociable, intelligent, playful, entertaining and lovable.

The first pigs we had impressed us with their strangely human personalities and their ingenuity at finding ways to avoid our attempts to restrain their freedom. Begrudging respect gradually evolved into admiration and eventually fondness, especially from Kiersten, who, just like her mom, was a born animal lover and their main feeder. This became quite a problem at butchering time. None of us were vegetarians, but we felt that if we ate meat at all we should experience what is involved in the kill rather than having someone else do the dirty work for us. The reward was a significant example of an important principle we learned about farming. It's always good to get two things for the price of one. With pigs we got three. The actual cost, including the feed we had to bring in, worked out about the same per pound as store-bought pork, but the pigs also did an amazing job of breaking up the raw land, loosening rocks and roots. They fertilized the land as well. We can still see many years later how there are fewer rocks and weeds in the areas where the pigs were.

After numerous botched attempts at slaughtering we finally arrived at a strategy whereby Laurie tempted the victim with a carrot to push its nose through the picket fence while I held the gun directly to its forehead and pulled the trigger. Then Laurie plunged the knife into the throat to start the bleeding.

Maybe this tells you something about our personalities. Laurie could never bring herself to actually kill the animal, but she didn't mind sticking the knife in and letting the blood, whereas I had no trouble with the shooting but could never stand sticking in the knife or the blood, even after the creature was dead.

We did the butchering when the weather was

cold in winter, and it involved hoisting the carcass on a tall tripod with a block and tackle above a 45-gallon drum of water boiled on an open wood fire beneath. We lowered it into the boiling water to soften the bristles so the hair could be shaved off. The sharp knife went in again to open up the carcass and remove the guts. Then came the carving and chopping. The final and best part of this whole complex procedure was eating the bacon and pork chops, which were undoubtedly more tasty than their store-bought equivalents and free of preservatives.

The second pair of pigs we bought were one-month-old piglets from a farm on the south end of Quadra Island. It was a hot midsummer's day and we had just taken delivery at Campbell River airport of my 13-year-old niece, Zandra, who was travelling from Halifax, Nova Scotia, for the first time away from her mum and away from the suburban lifestyle. Poor lass – she had no idea that what she was about to witness turned out, even by our standards, to be one of the most weird and wacky afternoons in all our years on the land. Talk about culture shock!

First thing was that part of the purchase deal was that the young piglets were loose in a pen about the size of two tennis courts and we had to play rugby with them for half an hour before catching them. Then we shoved them into gunny sacks ready for transport in the back seat of the car we had borrowed for the occasion. We had one caught, "in the bag," so to speak, with the window open because it was so hot. When we came back to the car with the second one, we discovered the first one had escaped out of the gunny sack and the car window and had taken off across the surrounding countryside. To cut the story short, we eventually caught it after an hour of really embarrassing invasions of people's privacy and an exhausting cross-country run and more aborted rugby tackles, but this time not even contained by the limits of a playing field or pitch.

Finally, after hours of chasing, we had them both in their gunny sacks sharing the back seat of the car with Zandra and Kiersten. Then we had the 45-minute boat ride up to our island in our aluminum skiff, fully exposed to the hot afternoon sun. While one of the piglets lay calmly in the bottom of the boat, the other one, the male needless to say, was banging its head nonstop on the side of the boat. Attempting to cool him down, the girls were busy pouring sea water over him. When we eventually pulled in to the beach directly below our homestead, Laurie immediately grabbed the male in his sack and sprinted off up the trail. I took the female at a more leisurely pace with the girls in tow.

Just a few yards short of the pen, to my surprise and to my poor niece Zandra's absolute horror, we came across Laurie lying on top of the pegged-out, belly-up male piglet, attempting to perform mouth to mouth resuscitation.

No luck. The pig, like Monty Python's parrot, had "snuffed it." It was an "ex-piglet."

"It 'ad met its mortal maker." The young skiers knew the lines.

So we packed the carcass up to our house and put it in the bathtub and sent a message with the girls to our neighbours, who were the most experienced farmers in the neighbourhood, to come and help butcher the piglet. Trouble was, these two farmers were also raving alcoholics who brewed their own moonshine. They were too drunk to come now but agreed to come next morning. They arrived first thing, already looped, brandishing and gesticulating wildly with their carving knives. Amid much hilarity on their part and ours but sheer panic on my niece's, they went through the whole butchering ritual. At one point, the plump farmer's wife warmed her hands up by putting them inside the carcass before pulling the guts out.

Sensing her cousin had had enough, Kiersten offered to take her over to visit some other girls and go horseback riding on the next island, only to find that the scene over there was even more mad than ours, at which point poor Zandra asked to be taken back to the airport.

Discussing the incident with her many years later, when she was an adult, I found she remembers the whole thing fondly and confided that she'd had the feeling, at the time, that she had to go home because if she stayed with us any longer she too would have become so crazy she would never have been able to go back to her normal life.

Perhaps we should say that we have since become more vegetarian than we used to be and no longer keep pigs.

Laurie has always insisted on having chickens.

Although I enjoy eating their bright yellow free range eggs, I have always been skeptical about the economic benefit of the effort. Although the flock finds much of its own food scratching in the yard and the woods, we supplement it with a couple of 25-kilogram bags of cracked corn every month, bringing it all the way from the pet store in town, into the car, then into the boat, then onto the tractor and then into the barn. In return we get close to one egg per chicken most days, except when they're brooding or moulting. Lauric usually has about 15 chickens and a rooster so we often have a surplus of eggs which she sells to neighbours.

The hens sleep lined up in rows on the roosts in their henhouse in the barn. At dusk they all come trooping home and line up quite peaceably by pecking order on the roost. They are sociable, and like to be where the people are, whether that's in the yard, on the deck, or in the house if we aren't careful. Laurie gets most of their attention, as they revere her as a main food source.

Once an old climbing friend called Pete Muscroft came to visit with his sarcastic and cynical sense of humour, and when I told him I had conversations with chickens he scoffed contemptuously. Then one day I was talking to a chicken that had wandered inside the house, suggesting that she scoot, and she was clucking politely in reply. The visitor was on the couch reading the newspaper.

"Hey Pete. The chicken's talking to you," I said.

"Oh yeah? What's she say?" he scoffed, putting his paper down condescendingly.

"Buck 'orff, Muscroft," I replied.

Chickens usually get taken out by one or another of a long list of predators before they grow old and die: hawks, ravens, owls, cougars, mink, weasels and neighbours' dogs. Mink are by far the worst because they will kill the whole flock and not even eat any of them. Yes, nature can sometimes be red in tooth and claw. Blue jays (Stellers) are a nuisance because they pinch the chicken feed.

One day I was over at the barn and saw Laurie squatting down and peeping out the back door.

"Whatcha doing?" I asked.

"Catchin' blue jays," she replied.

Then I saw the cardboard box out on the ground in the chicken run perched at an angle on a stick tied to a piece of string that led to Laurie's hand.

"Caught any yet?"

"Caught one."

"Whatcha do to it?"

"Clipped its wing feathers."

"So you mean it can't fly anymore?"

"It can still get around. If it does come in here again, I'll clip them some more."

"They're pretty smart."

"Too damned smart."

Once, when Kiersten was working at a local fish farm, part of her job was shooting predatory seals, which she really did not want to do. She came home after a ten-day shift one time and confided in me that she had had to kill a seal that day and was upset and worried about what Laurie would say.

"Don't worry about your mum," I said. "She just killed a mink in the chicken house with a piece of plywood this morning."

"You must have had dogs."

YES, OF COURSE. FOR MANY years we had a wonderful female dog called Sheen. A shepherd and malamute cross, she had originally belonged to our next door neighbours, and their young son had named her after her beautiful shiny white coat. She always knew exactly what was expected of her and never transgressed. Funnily enough, she took a liking to me. This was very flattering and hard for me to understand because I was notably disinclined to bond with animals, no doubt because I had missed out on that experience as a child. Sheen was so adorable that even I was softened by her spirit and allowed her to teach me unconditional love.

She went everywhere with me, including all kinds of adventures in our sailboat and in the mountains. On one occasion we had Kiersten, aged 8, and Sheen along with us on an ascent of a 9,000 ft. peak straight up out of the sea at the head of Bute Inlet. Everything went well on the ascent, but coming down we thought we'd take a shortcut which ended up requiring a rappel down a cliff. We showed Kiersten how to do it and gave her a makeshift harness and safety rope that worked out well enough, but poor old Sheen slipped out of her improvised harness and fell part of the way down the cliff, fortunately landing in soft snow. She took off on her own the rest of the way down the mountain. Hours later, she was waiting for us in the boat.

I was so used to her following me that I never had to think about where she was, but alas as she got older she sometimes gapped out, and of course so did I and didn't notice she was no longer with me. It happened in town one time when I went into a tool rental store and she patiently sat outside the store as usual. I came out, jumped into the car and drove all the way back home without her.

I found her next day still lying quietly outside the store where I had left her.

Although Sheen was a tough act to follow, our next dog, a big male shepherd called Skookum, possessed all of Sheen's qualities and more. Although he already had his name when we acquired him as a puppy, it turned out to be uncannily well suited to his character. The word "skookum," meaning strong, well integrated, well put together, is from the Chinook dialect, which was part English, part Native and part French, used universally across Canada by the first settlers and traders.

A big dog with natural equipment for delivering violence, he never did. On the contrary, his gentle, playful spirit and his insistence on enjoyment of the moment brought great joy to many people. He avoided fighting with other dogs and was sometimes timid and afraid of smaller ones. He was fascinated by cats but had his nose scratched a couple of times from getting too close to Irish too soon. He never forgave her for that. The closest he ever came to violence was popping balloons.

I remember one time at the Heriot Bay dock I had just finished carrying loads down the ramp from the car to the boat and was untied from the dock and ready to leave, except there was no Skookum. He was still standing at the top of the ramp and didn't show any sign of coming down when I called him. This was most unusual because he loved boat rides and was usually the first one into the boat. Looking around to see what was spooking him, I noticed a tiny little terrier at the bottom of the ramp that Skookum could have eaten for lunch if he had wanted to. I had to go all the way back up the ramp and bring him down whimpering like a puppy.

For those of us who were blessed with his companionship on a frequent basis, the quality that moved us even more than his Sheen-like loyalty and love was his extraordinary intelligence. He had a vocabulary of over 200 words, most of them toys. You could tell him to go fetch his dinosaur and he would run to his huge basket of toys, spill them all out on the carpet and sort though them with his long nose, pick out the right one and bring it to you. He was a master entertainer and revelled in the spotlight of attention. With the array of tricks that Laurie taught him, he sure could hold an audience. We had him at a party in Vancouver one time with a kitchen full of people jammed together. He entertained everyone for an hour with a spontaneously invented game of tapping a balloon up in the air with his nose.

In the bush he was right in tune and enjoyed tracking; in the mountains he was superb, agile as well as strong. We had him out on hundreds of great mountain trips, including numerous ten-day ski mountaineering expeditions into the Mount Waddington Range, pulling his own sled full of dog food on the way in and full of our garbage on the way out. He was always a star, not only in the entertainment department but also in safety. His herding instinct demonstrated obvious concern for the well-being of the group, and his awareness and sensitivity to the vibrations of the environment were a great source of security for us as well as an inspiration. He was always in the Zone.

One time, on a ski trip in the mountains, our friend Lyle was giving us a bit of a workshop on the use of avalanche transceivers. Lyle had previously buried an activated transceiver in the snow some distance away. When it came time for Lyle to stop instructing and send us off to find it, he was confronted by an excited Skookum with the transceiver in his mouth, poking Lyle with it in the crotch.

He was with us when we crossed the Hecate Strait to the Queen Charlotte Islands (now Haida Gwaii) in *Quintano*. Although this passage was very rough, it was also remarkably fast and we sailed the 72 miles in only ten hours. Even though Skookum would never go to the bathroom on the boat, this long day was not too much of a problem. On the way back, however, we took a more diagonal line across the strait that gave us a 130-mile passage, and because there was no wind, we had to motor. In order to conserve a limited fuel supply, we had to travel slowly, with the result that poor old Skookum went for 34 hours without a pee. Poor lad was not quite sure of his legs when he finally got ashore and headed up the beach to the grass.

On a lovely, sunny, spring-like day, but oh so sad, we had to lay our beloved old Skookum to rest in the garden. Needless to say, this was an extremely emotional time for us. I am brought to tears again, just writing about it now. A big dog in his fourteenth year, he had been deteriorating for some time, but about ten days previously, after he had not eaten for a few days, Laurie took him to see Marlene, our very good friend the vet. She diagnosed internal bleeding (probably from a ruptured tumor) and warned us that he was very close to the end. We thought it best to take him home to die peacefully in a day or two, but the old trooper hung in for another ten days. He was completely immobile toward the end, however, and Laurie was attending to him like a baby, complete with diaper changes in the middle of the night. Although he did not seem to be suffering too much, I could see that Laurie was, so I took Marlene up on her offer to come up to our island and put Skookum down with an injection. The time seemed right, as it was the first beautiful sunny day for quite a while.

Skookum showed me that animals can equal humans in many ways. Their body language is amazingly sophisticated and their ability to communicate honesty is staggering. It was never necessary for us to train him. He was so smart and learned so quickly, he always knew, telepathically, exactly what was expected, and his desire to please was so powerful he automatically tuned into the flow, from curling up and keeping still in boats to scrambling up rock faces. He didn't need training or regulating. With all sincerity and humility, I can honestly say that, rather than being his master, I considered Skookum an equal if not a superior being. I certainly consider it a great privilege to have been his friend. Through him I have learned to place my allegiance with the commonwealth of other creatures with whom we share this beautiful planet. He had a good life and one we will never forget.

Skookum sure was a skookum dog.

-8-

WILD ANIMALS

**"Do you ever see or hear any
wolves on your island?"**

WE USED TO HEAR THEM a lot when we first
came up, sometimes really close to our houses
but mainly at night, so we rarely saw them. They
haven't been around so much in recent years. Some
of them have unfortunately been shot. Wolves and
cougars don't share the same territory at the same
time and their presence in any one area alternates.

They both feed on deer, so the deer populations fluctuate quite dramatically in symbiosis. They all swim across the channels between the islands.

We once went to the next island to pick up a goose we had been given and were heading back home with Sheen dog, walking along an old skid road through deep second-growth forest. Laurie was carrying the goose and she had put a sock over its head to help keep it calm. Sheen was happily running along ahead as usual but suddenly she started whimpering and ran back beside us, obviously quite spooked. At the same time the goose started squirming and squawking. We looked ahead and there, only 20 feet away, right on the edge of the road and the bush, was a magnificent, huge bracken-brown wolf looking right at us. Once we had got over the shock we realized we were not afraid, though both the dog and the goose obviously were. I had time to notice how magnificently calm and dignified the wolf looked and how well it blended into the environment. It was not threatening, so we tried gingerly continuing on our way even though this meant we would have to pass closer to it. Sure enough the wolf turned away and allowed us to pass even though we could still see it in the bush alongside of us.

Then, when the dog and the goose started getting angsty again, we suddenly realized there were several wolves beside us. When we looked on the other side there were several more, and when we looked behind us we saw a single big black wolf following us along the road. Now we had no choice but to keep on going and our pace quickened up.

Trouble was, we were heading into a gully formed by erosion and wear and tear on the road by heavy logging machinery, which gave us the feeling we were being herded into a canyon trap. So we avoided it by leaving the road and following the upper rim of the trough, right on the edge of the bush. Now that we were committed, our adrenalin was really pumping as we involuntarily broke into a run. It was as if we were being escorted off the premises. We no longer looked around, just straight ahead. Sheen dog took off and sprinted ahead of us. After a while we needed to rest, and when we took another glimpse around the wolves had vanished. Once again, Sheen was waiting for us in the boat.

"What about bears?"

THERE WERE NOT SUPPOSED TO be bears on our islands, till one showed up and broke into somebody's house. Since then we've had a few, mainly in the fall when they come looking for apples.

We arrived home from a town trip one evening in the fall, just before dark, to see a gap in our garden fence. Laurie was ahead of me as we came into our clearing, and she was going right for the hole in the fence to check it out. She didn't want the chickens getting into the garden. As I arrived on the scene from a more distant viewpoint I was able to see over the fence and into the garden, where my attention was immediately distracted from the gap in the fence by a flurry of motion over in the apple tree at the far corner of the garden. As the flurry of activity emerged from the apple tree it took the unmistakable form of a bear cub right at the very top of the tree. Then a much more deliberate motion, a huge mama bear rearing up on her back legs. This mama was the biggest black bear I've ever seen. She must have stood at least eight feet tall. That and the brown colouring on her back made her look like a grizzly. The cub sure looked cute, I had time to notice.

Laurie was now at the fence, only the width of the garden, about 100 feet away from the bears and had evidently still not seen them, the fence itself being solid enough to obstruct her view. Suddenly mama bear set off running at great speed across the garden, directly toward the hole in the fence where she had entered, which was also right where Laurie was standing. I screamed at Laurie, "Run, there's a bear!"

At that point, only 20 feet from Laurie, mama bear stopped dead in her tracks, evidently sensing that junior was not following her, spun around on a dime and sprinted off back toward the apple tree. Meanwhile, the cub had decided to run the opposite way and, having just broken a new hole in the fence behind the apple tree, was heading toward our house, which also happened to be where I was planning on going ASAP. Mama bear sliced smoothly through the new hole that junior had just made in the cedar picket fence, caught up with the cub and ambled off past our back deck and disappeared into the forest, heading back toward our barn.

Unfortunately, Laurie was also heading to the barn, round the opposite side of the garden, no doubt to check on the chickens. So I screamed again to tell Laurie to come back around my side of the garden so we could get safely to the house. Laurie argued that she didn't want to go to the house. She wanted to make sure the bears didn't get her chickens. She headed for the barn. I followed my instinct to hide in the house and wait for them to go away, which, thankfully, they did.

I had already finished my first cup of tea when Laurie finally came in from the barn, the smile on her face indicating that she and the chickens were okay but now she was worried about the apples. She didn't want the bears getting any more apples.

"To hell with apples," I said. "Did you see how big that mama was, and how close she was to you?"

"I don't want the bears doing any more damage because then we'll have to call in the Wildlife Manager to come and shoot them," she replied, light years ahead of me in her strategic thinking as usual.

"So long as they don't come in the house," I thought. "I'm not going out and I don't care what they do tonight. I'll worry about the apples tomorrow, maybe."

As an adjunct to this part of the story, some of our neighbours on the next island at about the same time had a bear open their kitchen window, climb right inside their house, take a good look around and exit by the same means. They were away at the time and it did not do any serious damage or steal any of the plentiful supply of food in their pantry, including pails of honey and dozens of cans of salmon. Could it possibly have been the same bears? They also swim between islands.

There's another interesting sequel to this story too. A few days later we were having supper with some friends just about dusk when I happened to glance up from the dinner table as something caught my eye right through the back kitchen window at the far side of the house out toward the garden. It was that same damn bear cub again, right at the very top of that same apple tree. It's a huge tree and was just loaded with apples that we still hadn't got round to picking. Unfortunately, instead of doing the smart thing, which was to grab the camera, I ran out and shouted at them again. Sure enough they ran off and slid right through the original spot in the fence that Laurie had already repaired.

"How about cougars?"

THE FIRST MORNING BACK HOME from some travelling, Skookum was barking out by the barn. We had been missing each other, as he had been staying with Kiersten in town for the three months while we were away, and he was now keen to pick up his old routines, which included asserting control of his territory. He often barked at the ravens and blue jays. He knew we didn't want to have them around and chasing them away made him feel important, which of course met our approval, of which he also was acutely aware. His will to please was very powerful. Sometimes he overdid it, which then became part of his entertaining act, and he barked at nothing at all just for the hell of it.

This over-enthusiastic barking was not at all unusual, then, but this time, partly because we hadn't seen each other for months, there was something different so I went out to join him at the barn to see what was up. I thought I'd go through the motions of letting him save face before playing some other game, but somehow this time there was an urgency about his body language that really caught my attention.

"What's up, Skook?" I asked as he came close in against my legs.

Now I was starting to get spooked by his unusual behaviour, realizing this was not just a game, and even my skeptical senses were catching on to some other presence. As we both tentatively stalked along the lane, his nose suddenly poked upward, indicating he had caught a scent of something. Sure enough, just around the corner from the barn, only 50 feet away right in the middle of the lane, there was a huge cougar, a 150-pound mountain lion that could easily tear either one of us apart in the blink of an eye. Fortunately, she wasn't blinking, just staring, catlike and curious. Her body was facing away from us but her head was turned right around to the back of her neck the way only cats (or owls) can do. I was not afraid, nor was Skookum; there was more a feeling of mutual fascination, intense curiosity on both sides. I couldn't help noticing what a beautiful creature she was and how well she blended into the bush while at the same time presenting a very distinctive and powerful presence, almost an aura. She was big, muscular and fit-looking, about twice as big as Skookum (and he was a big dog), tan-coloured with some tabby stripes, a very big kitty. The body language was not threatening but certainly demanding of respect, especially the intensity of that expressionless gaze.

"Better not push our luck, old chap. Let's go back home now!" I said calmly to Skookum, and then I thought, "You are not supposed to turn your back on a predator."

Instead, the cougar turned its back on us and slunk off into the bush. We quickly slunk off back to the house. It was all over so fast with no time to consider the what-if scenarios.

Safely back in the house, it felt good to be home. We sure had missed our animals.

When people ask why we are not afraid of the cougars on our island, we say, "They seem to know not to bother us, so long as we don't bother them."

Although, of course, we can't prove it, this attitude has worked for us for 40 years of living with cougars in our neighbourhood. Although we rarely see them, we know they are there because whenever it snows we see their tracks. Furthermore, our seemingly cavalier attitude is substantiated by the local folklore passed down to us by the old-timers we have met. For instance, the daughters of August Schnarr, the local old-time pioneer homesteader, prospector and trapper living in Bute Inlet, had pet cougar kittens in their house when they were young.

When we were in Australia people asked us, "What about the bears in Canada? Aren't you afraid of being mauled and eaten?"

"More people get killed by bees than bears," we replied. "They are around and we see them now and again but they usually keep away. There's no need to be afraid. How about your poisonous snakes? Aren't you afraid of them?"

"Hell no. There's plenty of them around and you might see the odd one but they usually keep away. No need to be afraid."

"How about sharks and crocodiles?"

"Same thing, but you can't help being afraid of them."

Some people are afraid of horses, but the people who know them say that it doesn't help to be afraid. Respect is a preferable state of mind.

9

FIORDLAND BOAT

**"Why and when did you build
your catamaran, *Quintano*?"**

I HAVE OFTEN HEARD THE BC coast described as a
"high-maintenance environment," and we gradually
discovered that our abuse of *Shadowfax* exceeded
our ability to look after her properly and that we
were fighting a losing battle against rot. She ended
her life in a cremation ceremony on the beach in
which we were thankful for the five years of faithful

service she had provided and for the lessons we had learned. In other words she was written off to experience. So now what?

We figured out that what we needed was a fast, shallow draft sailboat, with great stability and load carrying ability, capable of serving as a work boat as well as for pleasure. I heard about two fibreglass outriggers from a Cross 38 trimaran that had been sitting in a shed in Campbell River for ten years. After checking them out we bought them for a very good price, lashed them together and paid a friend to tow them home to our island. We erected a pole structure on the beach with a tarp roof, and for the next two years it became the birthplace of *Quintano*, a 33-foot long, 14-foot wide and 2-foot deep catamaran.

As she was put to the test of ferrying huge loads of building supplies, dealing with winter southeasters and negotiating the local tidal rapids, we discovered that *Quintano* turned out to be a fine boat, well beyond what we had dared dream of or expect. She was fast and lively with tremendous acceleration but at the same time comfortable, stable and seaworthy. The shallow draft enabled us to go close in against the shore for loading and unloading and to get into more sheltered anchorages.

"Quintano" is the name the Spanish explorer Captain Quadra gave for Bute Inlet after one of his midshipmen, and for over 20 years she sailed the magnificent and challenging local waters, carrying climbing and ski mountaineering expeditions into the Mount Waddington area at the heart of the BC Coast Range.

"What was *Quintano*'s best adventure?"

EVER SINCE I HAD COME to the coast I had dreamed of going all the way around Vancouver Island, but having survived a few near misses, I had learned to keep my youthful headstrong impulses somewhat under control. It seems inherently part of my personality to underestimate practicalities. Perhaps that is just as well, because otherwise I would never have tried so many of the things I have done, including building *Quintano*.

One evening in August 1986 *Quintano* quietly slipped her moorage and motored out into the Okisollo rapids with the end of ebb tide, thereby fulfilling one of our favorite lessons learned in the wilds:

"Leaving home is the hardest part of any trip!"

This time it was especially true. What with the responsibilities of looking after our horse, pigs and chickens, work commitments and the fact that Laurie had an old friend from Alberta coming to visit, we did not really have enough time to go all the way around the island, but we would head up to Port Hardy and see what happened anyway.

Right at the northern and most remote end of Vancouver Island is a small island called Hope, for the very good reason that the narrow channel that separates it has a shallow shoal which, together with certain conditions of wind against tide, can present one of the most notorious hazards to navigation on the BC coast: the dreaded Nahwitti Bar.

This time there was, however, yet another formidable element to contend with – thick fog; pea soup.

Quintano motored timidly out of the narrow harbour mouth and clung closely against the shore of Hope Island, peering hopefully into the featureless grey gloom. Visibility was just enough to keep us clear of the rocks. It did not take long, even at slow speed, to reach the lighthouse at the western end of Hope Island, with its eerie foghorn and ghostly light. Beyond this was the point of no return. To proceed west toward Cape Scott, *Quintano* and its crew of Rob, Laurie, Kiersten and Sheen dog would have to leave the security of Hope Island, pass over Nahwitti Bar and head out into the open ocean – an ocean of fog. This was before the days of GPS, and even though we trusted the compass and had experience dealing with fog on the inside coast, we had never been out in the open ocean before.

Beyond the bar lay 20 miles of exposed lee coastline to Cape Scott, another notorious spot. After that we would head south in our bid to negotiate the west coast and complete our objective, the 650-nautical-mile circumnavigation of Vancouver Island.

Frankly, I was scared of that damn fog. I knew that I was wimping out and felt nauseous with indecision and fear. Slowly, we turned around and I tried to rationalize by muttering, "Let's try again tomorrow."

Having turned around, we were once again trying to pick out the rocky shore from the impenetrable grey gloom when Kiersten, our lookout on the bow, suddenly shouted, "Look! Look! A whale!"

A huge grey whale gently broke the surface

halfway between *Quintano* and the rocks. As if to confirm its presence (which one could have been excused for doubting considering the perfect camouflage of its grey barnacled back in the grey swell, the grey rocks and the grey fog), it let out, with a snort, a spout of grey vapour before rolling forward into the swells. Spellbound, we eagerly anticipated its rising for a repeat performance, which it soon obliged us with, this time even closer, exposing even more of its body and tail. We gasped as, almost right alongside *Quintano*, it turned its head toward us, showing a doleful and compassionate eye. I could have sworn it was smiling, even winking at us.

"A wink's as good as a nod to a blind bat." The Monty Python spoof came out aloud.

"Did you take any photies, eh?, Nudge nudge, wink wink?"

The apprentices were still listening.

"Look! Look! There's another one – two – three!" yelled Kiersten, more perceptive than me, again. "There are lots of whales!"

There were at least half a dozen grey whales all around us. I instinctively turned the helm to follow them back the way we had just come, toward the open sea. We were entertained by this playful exhibition of hide and go seek by the whales and switched the engine off so we could better hear their "blowing" and the swishing of their flukes. They were not at all threatening, even though at times they were only a few feet away from the boat.

As the novelty of watching the whales wore off, I started the motor and locked my focus onto the compass bearing: 225 degrees, 20 nautical miles, 3 hours and 20 minutes motoring at 6 knots. Time: 2:00 PM. Anticipated arrival at Cape Scott 5:20 PM.

I opened the throttle and *Quintano*'s bows cut smoothly into the ocean swell. Before I had chance for further reflection or doubt we had crossed Nahwitti Bar, lost sight of land and the whales and were out in the open Pacific.

We soon picked up a favourable breeze and *Quintano* surged forward at thrilling speed, sails wing-on-wing running straight downwind, carving smoothly into the sunny ocean swell. We had intended to stop for the night at Winter Harbour, but we were making such good progress, the weather was so fine and evidently stable, that we decided to continue on through the night while the going was good. As the sun went down to starboard a huge moon came up to port.

Everything went well until Solander Island off the tip of Brooks Peninsula, the farthest westerly point on Vancouver Island. We had changed course, having rounded Cape Scott at 1:45 AM. I was thinking what a rugged and impressive-looking fortress Solander was, with its lonely light, when suddenly, without warning, we entered chaotic, high-pitched seas with huge breakers bearing down on our stern. The wind picked up at the same time, whipping the water into white spray glistening in the moonlight all around. We were now running into the worst situation for a catamaran, with too much sail power, surfing too fast in huge following seas, with the possibility of having the bows dig into a trough and the boat tripping forward into a "pitch pole." As I rushed forward to pull the jib down, a monstrous breaking wave crashed over our stern and washed through *Quintano*'s cockpit, lifting Laurie right off her seat at the helm – "pooped."

Fortunately, in spite of the panic we felt and the intimidating predicament, *Quintano* remained steady and secure. Although, as they sliced through the chaos of white water both bows were often submerged, somehow the wing deck between the hulls was buoyant enough to lift us gracefully and comfortably out of the troughs. She felt more confident than we did, and that's a fine way to feel about your boat in a situation like this.

Lowering the jib seemed to make little difference. *Quintano* still hurtled along through the dazzling moonlit pandemonium. We needed to shorten the main. To do this, however, would have meant either "gybing" – swinging the boom across to the other side – a tricky and potentially dangerous operation at the best of times and totally unthinkable in these conditions, or else turning in toward the rocky shoreline to complete a U-turn to head up into the wind and spill the load off the main sail. Even though we were several hundred yards out, *Quintano* would travel extremely fast beam-on to the wind and could put us too close to the rocks too quickly. Anyhow, we didn't fancy being beam-on to these waves. The only possibility left was to heave the mainsail down, loaded as it was – a desperate and panicky measure.

I was busy struggling with battens caught up in the shrouds, no doubt cursing and swearing, pretty close to freaking out, when Laurie was pooped a second time. Thank goodness *Quintano* was easily able to deal with the problem by quickly self-draining the cockpit and, apart from the helmswoman getting soaked and spooked again, there was no serious effect.

Eventually, I managed to shorten the main and things started to settle down a bit. We felt more relaxed and even enjoyed the excitement and exhilaration of speed for a while before the wind and the waves suddenly eased off and left us wondering what on earth had been happening. "Like Hobbits at the gates of Mordor!" Laurie summed it up later.

Eventually, just about at dawn, we arrived safely in the welcome security of the remote First Nations village of Kyuquot among a fleet of fishing boats and stole a few hours of well-earned rest. Kiersten had slept through the whole thing, and when we told her about all the fun she had missed, she replied, "Good."

Things went relatively smoothly after that for the remainder of the voyage. *Quintano*, like a horse heading for the barn, beat up the last lap to the finishing line with spectacular speed and perhaps the most comfortably exhilarating sailing of the trip. As well as the normal satisfaction of getting where we wanted to go by using the wind without diminishing it, there was the additional thrill of riding a dynamic balance between speed and safety. The mechanical efficiency is fine-tuned with one hand on the tiller, responding to the sideways heeling thrust on the sails (safety), the other hand on the main sheets controlling the tension and shape of the sails (speed). It is precisely this intense participation in the flow of events, the interaction between ocean, wind, boat and man that moulds the rhythm of the sailor's thoughts and actions in harmony with the natural environment.

"In the Zone again. You must have felt exhilarated completing that trip!"

YES. WE COMPLETED THE 650 nautical-mile circumnavigation of the island in just nine days; that's an average of 70 nautical miles per day. We arrived home just in time to rescue one of our pigs that had broken loose from the pen and was hassling our neighbours.

Thanks largely to *Quintano*'s strength of character, we survived a wonderfully exciting adventure which, in the calmer light of retrospect, turned out to be one of the highlights of our lives and left us feeling a warm euphoric glow. The memory of *Quintano* surging through the ocean swells, the grey whales of Nahwitti and the white water of Solander will stay with us forever.

"Do you believe the whales of Nahwitti told you it was okay to proceed?"

I BELIEVE, AT LEAST, THAT our attention being focused on the whales connected us with the universal consciousness of the environment and that took us out of the subconsciously conditioned box of fear and doubt that had prevented us from proceeding.

"What happened to *Quintano*?"

THOUGH SHE HAD NEVER ONCE let us down and had carried us through countless adventures, I recently had a "senior moment" and carelessly left a piece of nylon cord smouldering in the cabin. The great Fiordland boat underwent a traditional Viking funeral when she went up in flames right down to the waterline while tied up at her home moorage in the same bay where she had been built and launched 25 years previously.

Quintano delivers visitors to Homathko Camp at the head of Bute Inlet. KAREN TONSETH

Hiking above Bute Inlet. KAREN TONSETH

BC Coast Range's "Deep Wilderness". ROB WOOD

Leaving home is the hardest part. BERYL KNAUTH

Yorkshire gritstone. WIL KING

Snowpatch Spire, Bugaboo Range. ROB WOOD

Shadowfax enters Desolation Sound. ORIGINAL PAINTING BY BILLY DAVIDSON

Pristine ambiance, Indian Paintbrush. PHIL STONE

Strathcona Park alpine magic. ROB WOOD

Northeast face of "Mystery Mountain" (Mount Waddington). DOUG SCOTT

Bivouac in a *bergschrund* (crevasse). JIM ALLAN

An outrageous apparition: The Tooth, Mount Waddington. DOUG SCOTT

Outer Islands school kids. GEORGE MANN

Mountains, the sea and me.
AUTHOR'S ORIGINAL LINOCUT

Co-op girls. DEBORAH KOZLICK

Quintano with our grandchildren, Ashley and Colton. LAURIE WOOD

Kiersten and Riskie on *Quintano*. LAURIE WOOD

Quintano's rest stop in Bute Inlet. ALIDA NUGENT

Discovery Islands. ROB WOOD

A cougar in the yard. CHUCK BURCHILL

Market Day at Outer Islands dock. JOANNE MCSPORRAN

Cowboy Hat, Discovery Islands. ROB WOOD

Our organic house. KIERSTEN RILEY

Our off-grid homestead. LAURIE WOOD

Wind Against the Tide: *Quintano* rounding Solander Island. ORIGINAL SKETCH BY LAURIE WOOD

Matt Maddaloni on the West Face of Mount Bute. JIM MARTINELLO

Looking out from the front deck. ROB WOOD

Rob and Laurie Wood on *Quintano*. ROSE COOK

Rob and Laurie Wood at home with Smokey.
KIERSTEN RILEY

10

MYSTERY MOUNTAIN

"Did you ever solve the mystery
of Mount Waddington?"

YES, BUT NOT WITHOUT HEAVY dues being paid
in a fascinating and exhausting investigation.

It was no coincidence that Laurie and I chose
to build our home right on the edge of the biggest
blank area on the road map of BC, so close to the
entrance to Bute Inlet as to be among the closest
permanent dwellings to Mount Waddington, some

80 miles to the north. Long before I arrived in BC, I had heard of the existence in the BC Coast Range of one of the world's great mountains, hidden in a barely penetrable shroud of remote and rugged wilderness.

As if we were attracted by the mysterious power of this archetypal legend, it soon became time for us to find out for ourselves some of the secrets of what the pioneering couple, Don and Phyllis Mundy, who first discovered the mountain as late as the mid-1920s, referred to as the "Mystery Mountain." Following their way, which was as they said, "more in the spirit of veneration than conquest," we made many trips into the mountain wilderness over the years, starting with a reconnaissance in *Shadowfax*, leading up to many ski mountaineering expeditions with *Quintano*, including one successful visit to the summit.

Initially Bute Inlet's coastal vista, though impressive and beautiful, is much like the rest of the lower part of the BC coast, with 6,000 ft. mountains. After you have cruised 45 miles to the head of the inlet with no sign of human presence, however, 9,000 ft. massifs rise high above the turquoise, glacier-fed waters. They form a vast three-dimensional panorama with steep forested shoulders, ramparts of vertical rock walls, hanging glaciers and sparkling snow-clad peaks. Sunlight shafts through the clouds, forming shimmering reflections in the final reach of the majestic fiord, which invert the whole magical scene and enhance even more the truly awe-inspiring grandeur which I have heard described as "Canada's Grand Canyon, except bigger and better."

Soaring high above the inlet, still almost 40 miles away up the Homathko Valley, the exceedingly graceful, 13,179 ft. (4002 m) spire of Mystery Mountain sparkles like a jewel in the sunlight. Though only a glimpse from this distance, its uncompromising presence stirs the innermost adrenalin reserves with tingles and shivers of excitement.

Bute Inlet's beauty is only one side of its moody and unpredictable personality. The other side, which can present itself without warning, consists of violent winds blowing up the inlet, down, or out of side valleys, funnelling and even spiralling the katabatic air currents into alarming and chaotic maelstroms. The long and exposed reaches provide ample "fetch" for the sea to kick up a devastating chop. The situation is made even more serious by the shortage of protected anchorages. Although there are a number of spots which are good for one direction, the wind is quite capable of switching.

Now it's time to find shelter and a safe place to leave the boat while we take off into the mountains. On this occasion, Laurie and I have a small group of six friends in *Quintano* with the intention of climbing the mountain in April. We had heard that living somewhere at the top of the inlet were some hand-loggers who might have a dock and be sympathetic to our cause. Sure enough, just a few miles down from the head, our binoculars pick out a lonesome cluster of buildings and a few boats tucked tightly in against the mountainside. They welcome us with impressive backcountry hospitality, gathered round a huge communal table, serving roast venison, home baking and all the booze we can handle.

"So much for surviving in the wilderness!"

They entertain us for most of the night with

Bute Inlet stories, mostly centring around two notorious old-timers, Schnarr and Parker, who worked in the inlet for over half a century. Living with their respective families on opposite sides and being the only inhabitants of the inlet, though they had once been partners, they hadn't spoken a word to each other for many years, even after one of their sons eloped with the other one's daughter.

Another story the hand-loggers tell us is about a Halloween party they had at their place in which most of the local loggers from the various camps around the head of the inlet were whooping it up and having a good time. It being late in the fall, they had been having early snow on the mountain and heavy storms with high rainfalls at lower altitudes. When one of them went outside for a pee, shortly before dawn, he heard and felt a loud rumbling coming from high up the steep mountainside above. It sent shivers down his spine and pierced his inebriated and befuddled mind with sheer panic.

"My God!" he realized, running back inside the house and screaming above the bedlam, "There's a slide coming down the mountain! We should all leave right now!"

"Ah, pull the other leg. It's got bells on," they all replied in unison.

"No! I'm serious! Come out and hear it!" he insisted.

Sure enough, they all soon got the message and ran down to the dock and into the boats just in time before a massive mud and rock slide took the deck right off the side of the house and hit the water with a thunderous splash that sent a tsunami out across the inlet. In the dawn light they could see bare stems of huge trees stripped clean of their branches popping up vertically out of the water like missiles all around them and hear the slide continuing to rumble in the depths below. Their dock, workshop, fuel tanks and the deck of the house had completely disappeared. The slide left a scimitar-shaped gouge 200 feet wide and 50 feet deep 5,000 feet down the mountain, pointing right at their place. Nobody was hurt but there was $20,000 worth of damage.

Next day we wait for the end of the flood tide before motoring into the Homathko Estuary. With the boat safely moored in a "hole" in the river, we hitch a ride with an empty logging truck 23 miles up the valley to Scar Creek logging camp, where we are wined and dined once again. The next day the loggers kindly run us up to the end of their roads, where with a cheery "Good luck!" they leave us, off and running on our own, looking directly into the jaws of a great granite gorge.

To get to the mountain we have a tough bush-whack ahead with no trail through the rugged canyon where the Homathko River carves a dramatic gorge from its source in the Interior Chilcotin Plateau, through the crest of the Coast Range to its delta at the head of Bute Inlet. Even though we know that the Chilcotin First Nations had a Grease Trail and August Schnarr had a trapline through to the interior, we are not aware of anybody in modern times having made it all the way through on foot.

Right from the start we are forced to make a 2,000 ft. detour up and over a band of bluffs that drop directly into the furious white water of the Homathko. Back down to the valley bottom, we camp on the river bank at a historic spot, the famous "Murderer's Bar" where Alfred Waddington's 1860s campaign to build a road linking Victoria with the interior gold fields ended with a bang.

A band of rebellious Native Chilcotins, led by the fierce warrior chief Klattasine, killed nine of Waddington's men. This incident triggered that inglorious chapter of BC's history known as the Chilcotin War.

Meanwhile, it takes us five days with heavy packs to thrash through the ten miles of bluffs, boulder fields, devil's club and lush virgin forest of the canyon and up a big glacier to our base camp at 6,200 ft. Dominating the scene is the intimidating grandeur of the 7,000 ft. northeast face of Mystery Mountain.

The weather is quite settled, so with four days' food supplies, stoves and fuel but no tents, we set off, expecting to climb the mountain in three days. After two days of really slow going in deep wet snow up the lower face, we make our second bivouac in a home-dug snow cave. Next day, in order to save weight, we leave most of our gear behind at the snow cave, but we are only partway up the Final Tower before nightfall. We are forced in rapidly deteriorating weather to dig into a crevasse at the base of the tower for an emergency bivouac (our third night), without much in the way of food, stoves or sleeping bags. During the night a fierce storm rages. Fortunately, the crevasse, though icy cold, offers shelter from the appalling weather. We huddle together to keep warm. Dehydration is now our biggest problem because without fuel we are unable to melt snow for drinks.

Doug, a highly experienced mountaineer, keeps our spirits up with tales of horrendous hardship in the mountains that help make our situation seem better than it is with expressions such as, "This is no bloody picnic!" and "Stay loose and hang in there!"

Next morning, the weather is still bad so, as we breakfast on the last of the cheese, a decision is made for Doug and I to retrieve the fixed ropes while the others set off down. Lauric will stay at the cave and wait for us. As we emerge from the crevasse, it is with mixed emotions, then, that Doug and I set off up the fixed ropes in thick cloud. We are glad to be moving at last, and ground conditions for climbing are good. I can tell Doug is thinking the same thing as I join him at the high point.

"So near and yet so far," he sighs.

"Yeah. We've come a long way," I reply. "I wonder if we'll ever get another go."

In spite of our weakness caused by lack of fluids, food and sleep, we have an impulsive urge to keep on climbing and find out what secrets of the mountain lie hidden in this veil of cloud. Suddenly, as we gaze longingly upward we both see at once a patch of blue.

"Let's go for it, youth," Doug adds impulsively. "Do we have time?"

"We could probably reach the summit and at least make it back to the crevasse," I figure.

Caught up in a rush of exhilaration, stoked by the release of all that pent-up frustration, I set off right away up a steep rock chimney choked with ice. Huge wind-carved ice crystal formations stick out horizontally from the rock. Shafts of brilliant sunshine pierce the clouds, illuminating distant peaks and glaciers and a nearby outrageous tooth-like spire.

Time races on and so does my exhaustion. The initial boost of energy I experienced earlier wears off, replaced by alarming spells of dizziness and a weakened ability to pull up, even on big holds.

Movements cease being planned with clarity and purpose. Numb hands now jam themselves into cracks. Legs brace themselves against sloping rock. Eyes grapple to focus on holds, as if hallucinating. Is it an optical illusion or a stage of physical exhaustion that presents the surreal apparition of the Tooth, poking up through cloud, floating Pisa-like high above the distant glaciers? The more I try to focus and give myself a reality check, the more the misty light plays tricks, causing the outrageous Tooth alternately to melt away into oblivion and then zoom closer and clearer.

In this dehydrated, exhausted and apparently altered state of consciousness, I experience the dazzling, sunlit mountain landscape as a flowing continuous process, the pulse of my body energy merging like liquid with the fluctuation of clouds, rock and snow. I become so immersed in it all that I can no longer be sure where the mountain stops and the sky starts, or where I stop and the mountain starts. In some strange, dreamlike way I am completely absorbed in the precarious beauty and wonder of it all. Thankfully, the rope fastens me to Doug, so we can't drift apart in the cosmic wind.

"Okay. Come on up." A very faint and distant voice penetrates the dream. My reluctant body forces itself into motion and once again it feels possessed by some weird surge of energy, which carries it up that final pitch. In spite of piercing pain, agonized breathing and every fibre calling out for rest, the body somehow automatically works its way upward. The mind seems separate, looking on as an observer from a distance away, voicing encouragement and support.

"Up you go. That's good. Up again. Move that foot up there. Now that hand. There you go!"

Slowly my conscious mind comes back into my body as the angle eases, though the exposure is formidable. There's Doug just up ahead, sitting in the sun with nothing but intensely blue sky above him.

"He's at the top." Thoughts focus. "We've made it."

I crawl on my hands and knees up those last few feet to join Doug on the tiny, precarious summit. We quickly and quietly embrace each other, then sit back in the snow, grinning. Our overstimulated perceptions attempt to absorb and savour the magnificent perspective. Layers of vaporous clouds below are punctuated by sparkling peaks and glaciers like jewels, with beams of intense sunlight shafting through from the deep space blue sky above.

Slowly our attention focuses on the 40 miles-distant inlet we had left ten long days ago, where our boat, we hope, is waiting for our return. There is the Homathko Valley and the 20 long miles of Tiedeman Glacier up which we'd skied. Base Camp is down there somewhere, tucked right underneath us. We search the lower slopes and find the tiny black dots which are our friends making their way down. Hopefully Laurie will be waiting for us at the ice cave and still speaking to us.

"It's four o'clock," said Doug, breaking the spell. "Sure could use a brew."

"Yeah. Me too," I reply. "Let's get on down. Then we'll get our brew."

II

DEEP WILDERNESS

"What is it about Canadian wilderness
that is so important for us to defend?"

SINCE EARLY CHILDHOOD I HAVE been intuitively responsive to the ability of wild places to affect my feelings and state of mind. In the old country, the landscape was often beautiful because it had been "cultivated" for thousands of years by people (and sheep) who were more in harmony with nature, but its power was diluted and tamed in comparison to the pristine Canadian wilderness. The crags where we climbed were more powerful than the surrounding areas because they had not been worked over so much. By comparison, our home island on the BC coast, though relatively wild and beautiful, has been modified by logging and lacks the potency of the pristine landscape of the more remote, rugged and inaccessible parts of the BC Coast Range.

My first conscious experience of deep, uncompromised wilderness was in 1971, when the famous British climber, Doug Scott, and I met in a Cairngorm pub and devised a plan to climb clean granite rock walls somewhere far away from societal distractions. We wanted to experience the pure spirit of exploration and self-reliance free from the bureaucracy, commercialism and crowding of popular places like Yosemite and Banff National Parks. We found that isolation in abundance in the mountains on Baffin Island in the eastern Canadian Arctic, where magnificent granite peaks, glaciers and treeless tundra bathe in the crystalline clarity of magic arctic light. After spending six weeks in this pristine landscape with complete absence of societal noise and clutter, we became increasingly conscious not just of the pretty view but also of a subtle ambient presence, a vibration that interacted and resonated with our feelings and emotions. Beauty became love.

We learned that things went better when we paid attention to these feelings and tuned into the surroundings and each other; when we listened and read the natural signs with our body/minds open and free. Then meaningful coincidences (synchronicities) and intuitive hunches happened more frequently, assisting our judgment and critical decisions, especially those concerning navigation, timing, weather and avalanches. Conversely, things went badly when we were not paying complete attention to our surroundings and each other; when our minds and spirits were distracted and out of focus. Deep wilderness experience taught us that our well-being, safety and ability to survive depended on conscious awareness of our internal and external environs.

In Strathcona Park, on Vancouver Island, I discovered a unique and particularly powerful version of the hidden connectivity of wilderness ambience. In the alpine areas between the steep, forested valleys below and the barren tundra of the high peaks and glaciers above, an extensive web of interconnected ridges provided relatively accessible, multi-day hiking expeditions through exquisite pristine meadows with exotic flowers and shrubs and sparkling streams and small lakes.

A dramatic example of the way this subtle energy of the pristine landscape can inspire love and conscious awareness and can move and shake us was demonstrated by the political battle to save this magical wonderland from the ravages of heavy metal mining in the late 1980s.

It all started for Laurie and me when we worked part time as wilderness guides for Jim Boulding at Strathcona Park Lodge & Outdoor Education Centre on Vancouver Island, leading hundreds of multi-day hiking journeys through the alpine paradise. Jim had been a great hunting and fishing guide, but when he discovered that killing game was not what his clients enjoyed, so much as the art of stalking (the state of mind of the hunter), he and his wife Myrna converted their hunting and fishing lodge into an outdoor education centre. Their mission was to teach people how to be more in tune with nature.

Jim was a big man with great charisma and a very commanding presence. You could say he had psychic power, with an uncanny shaman-like habit of thinking outside the box. Furthermore, he encouraged and instructed his staff to do likewise.

"The school classroom," he said, "was an architectural expression of the box mentality, the root cause of most of the problems of modern society."

Jim demonstrated the joy and power of sharing inspiration gained from interacting with the energy fields of the land in what he called "Generosity of Spirit." When we share the "Natural High" and the experience of "being in the Zone," the energy feeds on itself synergistically and amazing things can and do happen. Examples of this synergy are manifest in the safety record of the wilderness trips and the spontaneous music and dancing, organic architecture, delicious wholesome food and hospitality of "The Lodge." Jim's creation of Strathcona Rural Resource Village was as close as I ever came to a manifestation of my own thesis: a village on the edge of a protected wilderness park providing services, facilities and information for visitors outside instead of reducing the wilderness value by developing inside the protected areas.

According to Jim, "there are two types or outdoorsmen: Happy Warriors versus Whiners and Bitchers." I interpreted the latter to mean holding our own subliminal fears in abeyance by being fully focused and grounded in the moment and taking full responsibility for the consequences of our attitudes and behaviour.

Part of that responsibility, which he practised to a high degree himself, was what he called "stewardship of the land." Jim and others had been fighting successive waves of despoliation of Strathcona Provincial Park by government-sanctioned industrial resource extraction, mostly without success, since its inception in 1911. When, in the mid-1980s, the BC government of the day announced plans to open up 25 per cent of BC Parks, including Strathcona, for more mining and logging, on top of financial difficulties of running the lodge, it all became too much and Jim succumbed to pancreatic cancer. The Orwellian vision of what such government policy might mean for the future of society moved me to pledge to Jim, in his final days, that

I would do everything I could to continue his opposition to such a world.

Fortunately, I was not alone in my pledge of allegiance to Jim and the park. My old friend Stevey Smith and his wife Marlene also picked up Jim's baton and vowed to run with it. They too had spent many days hiking in the park and shared the love and inspiration for the subtle vibrations of the deep wilderness environs. Marlene described that feeling as "having your spiritual batteries charged."

Like David confronting Goliath, we never imagined we could win the battle, but neither could we stand by and watch our mother being raped; we were compelled to do something. So we started a citizen's action organization called "Friends of Strathcona Park" which soon enlisted huge support from all the communities surrounding the park. A Courtenay contingent organized a rally, attended by 600 people, with speakers emphasizing the spiritual, physical and mental health value of wilderness as well as clean drinking water. Others spoke to the economic value of tourism. A Campbell River group organized a peaceful "sit in" that blocked the highway through the park and temporarily stopped the trucks coming out of the existing mine. This "direct action" attracted the attention of the media and the event was broadcast on province-wide prime time TV news. At a huge demonstration on the lawn of the legislature, in Victoria, 50 blue herons circled overhead.

When "exploratory drilling" started, we organized a permanent camp vigil near the site, even though it was midwinter with challenging weather conditions. On weekends we formed a human chain around the drill rig, preventing its operation. When the police arrived to remove us there were volunteers who refused to leave. They were arrested and taken off to jail. All this drama was captured on live TV over a period of several months, and each time we had the opportunity to broadcast our message. We taught the cameraman how to keep warm and dry, and even he was inspired by being present on the land. That may have come across on the TV, because the sight of all of these decent-looking people being arrested caught the public's imagination, and when they heard our message support for our cause escalated dramatically. Particularly effective in this regard was the sight and sound, as each arrestee was dragged away by the police, of one of one our elders, a very dignified old lady, Ruth Masters, playing, "Oh Canada, we stand on guard for thee" (slightly off key), on her harmonica.

When public opinion polls indicated that as many as 75 per cent of British Columbians wanted their parks protected, the government backed off and withdrew their policy of downgrading not only Strathcona but all of BC Parks. The subsequent government increased the proportion of the land area of the province in parks from 5 per cent to 13 per cent and consolidated their protected status.

All this did not come about by chance or good luck. There was a phenomenal amount of voluntary hard work, many sleepless nights, vast numbers of phone calls, strained family relationships, time away from work and meetings, endless meetings. Tremendous sacrifices were made. Decisions were made by consensus and we used the First Nations method of keeping order by passing the speaking stick. We used Jim Boulding leadership techniques we had honed in the mountains to promote and maintain group synergy – when to push hard and go for it and when to back off and listen. Fortunately, as the protest escalated, new leaders emerged to help relieve the burnout syndrome. We received fantastic support from the environmental network and First Nations. One Native elder addressing a rally in the park said, "If we destroy our environment, we destroy ourselves."

Throughout it all, we were unquestionably guided and motivated by the unifying effect of the love we all shared for the land. Those of us who led this rare environmental victory have no hesitation in attributing the success to the survival imperative of Gaia (the living organism of the earth and its biosphere) expressing itself through our unconditional love for the park, which then synergistically resonated with the collective consciousness of British Columbians.

CANCER

"You must have had some setbacks
over the years. What were the worst
things that happened to you both?"

"WELL, LAURIE HAD BREAST CANCER. That was
pretty bad!"

At the end of a ten-day skiing expedition in the
Waddington Range, *Quintano* had just pulled in
to our dock with a boat full of ecstatic guests. As I
stepped off the boat, Laurie greeted me with the

news that "the results of the tests were positive!"

Breast cancer came as a complete surprise. Surely nothing like the big C thing could possibly be happening to Laurie of all people. She was always so fit and strong. It took us quite a while to get used to more and more bad news that took us progressively further down a road we had never wanted or expected to travel. It was like being out in a storm, always thinking the weather would get better but then having it just get worse and then worse again. So we had to adjust and adapt.

First, there was a "suspicious" lump, but it might have been benign. No, the biopsy proved it was cancer, so she had to have surgery, which removed not just one lump but two, and which also showed that the cancer had spread to the lymph nodes. This meant that it was not just Stage One cancer, as we had hoped, but the more serious Stage Two. By the time we got to the bottom of the bad news, Laurie was getting numb to suffering. When the female oncologist said, "The first surgery has not left a clear margin and, though a second surgery may be sufficient, we recommend a complete mastectomy," her emotional floodgates opened and she experienced the full depths of the despair that makes this such a fearful disease. To give the specialist credit, she gave Laurie the choice and allowed her overnight to think about it.

Next morning, to my amazement, she got on the phone and told the specialist she didn't want a mastectomy but would gamble on the second surgery being enough. This time the positive thinking paid off and the second surgery showed a clear margin. We had finally reached the end of the bad news. Laurie's intuitive decision had been right. The storm wind had changed and now she was finished with diagnosis and ready to start treatment and recovery.

Because the cancer had metastasized, chemotherapy was required to flush it out of the blood system. This was almost as frightening as cancer. Four three-week courses of an injected cocktail of heavy-duty drugs were prescribed to kill any cancer cells roaming around her body. Unfortunately, there was massive collateral damage, as it also killed all the other fast-growing cells, including all her hair and white blood cells, which are such an important part of the immune system. As well as making her vulnerable to infections, it induced dizziness, vomiting and exhaustion. About this time, we had a visit from Laurie's cousin Cathy who, by a strange coincidence, also had breast cancer and was also doing chemo. They made each other laugh by goofing around with various fancy wigs and hats. They started what Monty Python would have called "The Ministry of Silly Wigs!"

It was winter and there was a heavy flu epidemic happening in town so we were staying very close to our remote island home except for the routine visit every three weeks to the hospital for another hit of chemo. We had a scary period when Laurie picked up a dose of the flu right at the worst time in the cycle, when her immune system was at its lowest ebb. She was laid up in bed with a high fever, tossing violently from one uncomfortable position to another and coughing so hard that it strained her diaphragm. Living where we do on a remote island, we could not simply call an ambulance or drive to the hospital. The doctors agreed that we were better off on our germ-free island so long as we could get in to town quickly if we had to. Normally, we could make it within a couple of hours, and even faster with an emergency helicopter evacuation, but now our anxiety was heightened by a raging storm preventing any prospect of getting to town quickly. Even helicopters can't fly at night in really bad weather.

I had done as much as I could think of in the way of nursing and was alarmed by her increasingly high fever and deteriorating condition. Even through the previous months of successive bad news, she was pretty good at looking after herself and not letting things get her down, but now she was starting to lose it and was reaching out to me for help. Nursing did not come naturally to me and I was frantically running around trying to figure out what I could or should be doing. As a last resort, I came and sat on the bed holding her hand. I was desperately trying to calm myself as well as her.

"Let's try taking some deep breaths," I suggested as a particularly strong gust shook the house and rain splattered against the roof right above our heads.

"I can't," she gasped, "it hurts too much."

"Just listen to that rain," I said, nervously filling the silence as much to ease my own anxiety as anything else.

As we both concentrated on the sound of the rain spattering on the roof and the wind shrieking in the trees, the orchestra of sound alternately ascending and diminishing with all the drama and intensity of a Beethoven symphony, it gradually absorbed our attention and lifted us out of our predicament.

"Just like being storm-bound in a tent in the mountains." I reminded her of times we had had together, precariously exposed to severe weather conditions, unable to go anywhere or do anything to improve the circumstances. Resigned to conserving energy by attempting to relax and go with the flow, we had experienced a blissful dream world halfway between wakefulness and sleep and had often joked about how people in California paid big bucks for that kind of therapy known as "lucid dreaming."

"Better be a good tent," she murmured as the coughing stopped. I was mightily relieved to see a faint smile cross her face as she drifted off to sleep.

Next morning the fever was down, the sun came out and she was up and about and back to telling me what to do.

On another occasion, near Christmas with short days, we headed into town for the last chemo injection. In the middle of the day I left her at the hospital for her hour-long treatment while I blasted off to do the shopping so we could beat a hasty departure back home to our island before dark and also get her away from the hospital and town germs as quickly as possible.

As we started the return journey the sky darkened and it started to snow. As we drove up the 15-mile-long remote dirt road on the next island to ours, the snow was accumulating fast and suddenly there was an articulated truck jackknifed across the road, completely blocking it. After considerable messing about trying to help the truck driver move the damn thing, we decided to put the chains on our jeep and four-wheel drive her nose down into the ditch to get around the truck. This went well but we were losing a lot of time and it was already starting to get dark.

Although we could drive the boat the two miles back to our island through the tidal rapids in the dark, the prospect of a snowstorm blocking visibility altogether was extremely daunting. Worse still, the snow was really piling up on the road, and of course there was no snowplow and there were no tracks because no one else had gotten around the truck. Normally, the prospect of spending a night out in the back of the station wagon, even in winter, did not faze us because we were used to that sort of thing, but with the possibility of Laurie getting chilled, it was unthinkable. Now there was so much snow accumulating on the road that we were starting to worry about the jeep high-centring 12 miles out in the sticks with another four to go. Then, suddenly, there was a big alder tree down across the road. This time there was no way round it.

"Okay. That's it. No chance of getting home tonight and no chance of driving back to town, so now what?"

Fortunately, we had some friends who lived two miles back down the road, and we parked at the end of their mile-long driveway because we didn't want to risk getting stuck in there. By this time it was pitch dark and snowing like hell as we bundled up and started wading through knee-deep snow down the long, narrow driveway through the forest using a Bic lighter as a flashlight. Branches were snapping like machine gun fire all around us in the forest as great dollops of wet snow came crashing down like avalanches. Heads bent to the storm, arm in arm we soldiered on and eventually saw the lights of our friends' place. Thank goodness they were home and answered the doorbell.

"Ho, Ho, Ho!" we laughed, mightily relieved.

"Happy Christmas! Come on in." Just as if it were the most normal turn of events. "You're just in time for dinner!"

They laid out two extra places and we laughed ourselves into the blissful warmth and safety of their nice, warm king-size guest bed. Next morning they ran us back home to our island in their boat, and I went back for our car a few days later.

As the days got longer and spring came on, our spirits rose and Laurie's strength came back along with her hair. By the time she had to go down to Vancouver for an 18-day session of radiation, she was ready for some rock climbing therapy; radiation in Van in the mornings, climbing at Squamish in the afternoons.

While Laurie was taking on this challenge I had been reading Bernie Siegel's book *Love, Medicine & Miracles*. In it he describes how he discovered that approximately 15 per cent of his patients got better, regardless of what he as a mainstream physician did or did not do or say. Similarly, another 25 per cent would not get better regardless of what he said or did. Rather than quitting practice, which was his initial response, he decided to research why this should be the case. He came to the conclusion it was the placebo effect. Some people believe strongly enough that they can get better that they do so. They take responsibility for their own well-being, which has a very beneficial therapeutic effect. Further research indicated that this kind of conviction can only happen with high self-esteem, which in turn depends on loving support. The people who believe they will not get better do not experience loving support and are not able to take responsibility for their own well-being. This phenomenon is reminiscent of Jim Boulding's "Happy Warriors versus Whiners and Bitchers."

No one who knows Laurie had any doubt, and

least of all her, that she would recover, and she has in fact done so. With a lot of help from friends, family and community support groups, as well as the Canadian medical system, she's now well past the critical five-year test for long-term survival.

-13-
AORTA ATTACK

"Bravo, Laurie! What did Rob do to beat that?"

"HE DAMN NEARLY DIED. IN fact he did die, several times in one day," she answered.

Several years after Laurie's cancer, it was my turn to suffer a very serious illness: a ruptured aorta put me at death's door. Apparently, during an epic evacuation from our island home, 12 hours in Campbell River hospital emergency room, and eight hours of open heart surgery at the Royal

Jubilee hospital in Victoria, I went partway through that door several times before a medical miracle brought me back to tell the tale.

About nine o'clock one September morning I was alone down on *Quintano*, tied up at our dock, when I was hit with an intensely sharp pain inside my chest. I managed to stumble backward onto the bunk inside the cabin. Although the pain eased as I lay down, I was sweating profusely and felt wickedly dizzy. I knew right away that I was in big trouble. All I could think of was how to get Laurie to help me. The marine VHF radio was right above my head and for once I had the right piece of equipment, in working order, at the right place, at the right time. Without hesitation, I reached up and turned it on to Coast Guard Channel 16 and called a marine emergency distress signal, "Mayday, Mayday, Mayday!"

I gave my name and location, told them I was having serious chest pains and asked them to phone Laurie to coordinate further help.

It turned out that a neighbour up channel heard the Mayday call and phoned Laurie before the Coast Guard did. In what seemed to me like no time at all, a bunch of people, including Laurie and Fern, the neighbour who had phoned, showed up, and very soon a big military helicopter that had trouble finding a place to land. Luckily for me, it was low tide at the time and the chopper was eventually able to land on the beach close by. I can remember seeing it manoeuvre backward into the beach and put down four hydraulic legs like a giant insect. The neighbours congregating at the dock lifted me into a small boat and took me over to the other side of the bay and then, as if in a scene from "M.A.S.H.," the military dudes bundled me into the chopper like a sack of spuds and off we went to town. Less than one hour from the initial incident we landed at Campbell River hospital.

I noticed that it took forever after the engines had shut down on the helicopter pad at the entrance to the emergency ward before anyone came out to get me. It turned out the paramedics were on strike and would not cross the "picket line." Eventually two emergency room doctors pushed a gurney out and took me in. That's about the last thing I remember for the next two days.

Incidentally, I subsequently heard that the

same helicopter, just one hour later, had to do an emergency ditching into a lake because its main transmission had failed.

Then I went through a very serious 12 hour medical ordeal in Campbell River emergency room during which they had trouble figuring out the problem. I had a lot of the symptoms of a major heart attack and yet they could not find anything wrong with my heart. Having concluded after six hours of tests that I had had a "silent" heart attack, they gave me a blood thinner, at which point, apparently, my eyes rolled, I turned blue and my blood pressure dropped off the scale. "Upsydaisy."

This alarmed the ER doctor enough for him to jump outside the box and come up with an intuitive guess as to the correct diagnosis, which turned out to be a very rare and almost always fatal condition described medically as a "Dissected Aorta." The ruptured lining of my aorta was not only constricting the primary arterial blood flow, it was leaking blood into the cardiac sac and putting increasing external pressure on my heart, thereby steadily decreasing its function. So it then became a race against time to get me down to Victoria's Royal

Jubilee Hospital for surgery. But first they had to stabilize me enough to survive the helicopter air ambulance (AA) flight.

The AA chopper eventually left Campbell River about ten o'clock that night. Apparently it was touch and go whether I would survive the journey but I did. They had trouble finding a surgeon at short notice, but the one they found told me later that he was just out in the park walking the dog when he got the call. He actually called Lauric, who was being driven down to Victoria by some friends at the time, to ask her permission to operate on me. He said he would phone in the night if there were any problems. If she didn't hear anything she should show up for visiting hours at nine in the morning.

Open heart surgery started at 11 o'clock that night and lasted eight hours through the night. They had to completely replace three inches of the ascending aorta with a Dacron graft and also repair the aortic valve in the heart. This required not only bypassing the heart but also bypassing the heart/lung bypass machine by freezing my body down to 20°C. This cooling closed my whole circulatory system down except the very core of my brain, into which they pumped oxygenated blood through a peripheral artery in my shoulder. They almost lost me a couple of times because after they had completed the stitching job, reconnected everything and started the heart up again, the graft was still leaking and they had to start the whole bypass procedure all over again, twice.

When Laurie, Kiersten and my sister showed up at the intensive cardiac care unit for visiting hours at nine o'clock next morning, there I was, unconscious and full of tubes, with a nurse at the bedside working full-time on monitoring all the life support systems. Against only 3 per cent odds of survival, I was still alive.

The same time on the following day, I was sitting up in bed smiling, totally oblivious of my narrow escape, and everyone who came in saying, "Gee, you look great!"

"Huh?" I replied. "What's going on? Why shouldn't I be looking great?"

Many people ask if I had any profound revelations from my near-death experience. There was nothing dramatic. After all, I was unconscious through the worst of the crisis, and after I woke up, I was still heavily drugged. Apart from a few sleepless nights tormented by hallucinations, I was infused with very positive feelings of security and well-being that, like the hallucinations, were no doubt induced by the pain-killing morphine. However, during the eight days I was in the hospital, as I was weaned off the heavy drugs and became more aware of what was going on, I became increasingly impressed by another source of well-being and security: the technical proficiency and the dedicated care of the hospital staff, well above and beyond the call of duty.

I particularly remember an incident on day three of my stay in the cardiac ward of the Royal Jubilee Hospital. I had just had a phone call from my oldest sister in Halifax, Nova Scotia. She had offered to help pay our bills so Laurie and I did not need to worry about that end of things for a while. I was suddenly overwhelmed by such a powerful wave of emotion that I was shaking with a fit of uncontrollable weeping and sobbing. There happened to be a male nurse close by who came and sat on my bed. Embarrassed, I was trying to apologize for my crying.

"Don't you worry about crying," he said with a strong East Indian accent, "It's perfectly natural. After such a life-threatening, near-death experience, your hormones and emotions are all over the map. That's quite normal you feel like you have been born again." That cheered me up right away.

"Where you from?" he continued.

"Up near Campbell River," I replied.

"No. No. Where are you really from?"

"Okay. Yorkshire," I countered without hesitation

"Oh my God!" he retaliated, "That's Geoffrey Boycott country!"

Boycott is Yorkshire's and England's most famous cricketer.

"I never saw him play," I conceded.

"You didn't miss a thing," he proclaimed in mock derision.

At that point my breakfast tray arrived, and lifting up a lid he proclaimed with even more derision, "Oh my God, it's porridge! I can't stand the smell of it. I had too much of the stuff at boarding school in India, and don't mention pudding."

So deeply moving was the wave of humanitarian

empathy embedded throughout this conversation that it will stay with me a long time.

The number of well-wishing phone calls, emails, cards and visits I received was surprising. I had no idea people cared about me so much. There's no doubt in my mind that this incredible dedication of the Canadian rescue and health care system and the loving support from family, friends and community had a lot to do with my survival and initial recovery from this horrendous ordeal. I did not exactly see any bright lights, but on the other hand, I can't believe that what everyone agrees was my extraordinary survival was just a matter of luck or random chance. I'm sure there's a lot more to it than that.

No one can endure the kind of life-threatening illnesses that Laurie and I did without some serious soul searching, especially concerning the central questions of cause and prevention of recurrence.

We didn't know what caused the breast cancer or the torn aorta or if there was anything about our life that we could or should be doing differently. On the surface it's hard to imagine a healthier lifestyle and diet than ours. We ate more fresh fish and vegetables than most people, and Laurie, at least, was always so positive, cheerful and active. You had to know her really well to have noticed any suffering or unhappiness. Even though there was a history of some breast cancer in the family, including her mum, apparently it did not stack up as a worse than average predisposition to the disease – and yet somehow she got it. We both felt the cancer and the high blood pressure, possibly in some degree a genetic predisposition, were most likely caused by some uneasiness inherent in our lifestyle. Something in our lives must have been out of balance.

We have always been aware of the potential danger of too much self-reliance, which, while rewarding the natural self, can starve the social or cultured self, resulting in isolation and social poverty. It was not uncommon in our neck of the woods to see people with "cabin fever" who were "bushed": individuals who spent too much time alone or couples who had difficulty maintaining vitality and freshness in their relationships, especially when confined indoors together for long periods during the dark winter evenings.

We had to admit that our personal relationship might have been getting a bit rusty as many of our co-op neighbours had drifted away from the island not to return, except as occasional summer visitors. Although the community continued to exist, it had become geographically scattered. The kids remained close friends but they rarely came together on the land anymore. Laurie and I are now the only remaining year-round residents. I had always wanted to live in a village, albeit a remote one, but an isolated homestead was not the ideal we had bought into in the beginning. We now suffered from a disappointing isolation and a lack of resonant social energy to recharge our batteries. The personal difficulties it engendered between the two of us may well have contributed to significant deficiency in the wellness that can be derived from a loving environment. The health crises rocked us both out of our complacency, however, and taught us not to take for our love for granted.

An additional cause of frustration was our increasing economic dependence on the system. The downside of living adventurously out on the edge is the economic uncertainty, which we admit was very stressful. Being self-employed, and only partially so at that, we never knew where our next dollar would come from. In the past we had lived a very rustic and materially Spartan lifestyle. In other words we were voluntarily poor. Since the other folks around us were equally poor it never seemed to matter except when we went to town, which we rarely did. Part of our managing to stay on the island while other people had left, however, was due to our succeeding in making ourselves more comfortable, though still living strictly within our means without any debts or subsidies. Although we had more income these days from my increasingly successful home-based design practice, it meant more running into town and back as well as more responsibilities and stress. Striking a healthy balance between dependence and independence was easier said than done.

As soon as we could we took the opportunity of a long holiday abroad to focus on these central questions, to reflect on the lessons we have learned from living close to nature and to read up on some possible alternative new directions for ourselves as well as for society.

Inspired by hot tropical beaches and cool mountain breezes, we returned home with a renewed sense of commitment to the self-sufficient lifestyle but with a much broader understanding of what we meant by "self." We concluded that far from the conventional idea of rugged and independent individuals, our true self-reliance resided in our connectivity with both our social and natural world. Our new-found conscious intention was to strengthen all the various relationships that make up our field of care, our love.

14

OUTER ISLANDS COMMUNITY

"What kind of community do you have now?"

FORTUNATELY FOR US, JUST AS our co-op
community was fizzling out, the larger but still
local outer islands community, centred around the
school, the post office, the community centre and
the dock on the next island continued to flourish.
There still remain a lot of year-round residents,
and quite a few newcomers have arrived who have
chosen to live in the area mainly because of the

natural beauty and the lure of the off-grid lifestyle. Funnily enough, some of them keep on having children, so the presence of the community school is still a strong attraction.

Unlike our co-op, which started with grand ideological aspirations that couldn't be sustained, the outer islands community has evolved smoothly and continues to thrive because it has, at its core, not so much ideology as live experience of sharing both the natural beauty and the inherent adventure of travelling on the water and through the forests. Consequently, when people congregate at the centre they invariably bring some of the natural high energy, as well as humility, that comes from engagement with the wild natural environment. Everyone is keen to help others when they are in trouble, especially on the ocean, because they know that next time it could easily happen to them. We all look out for each other. Living off grid is not so much about solar panels and baking bread as about paying attention and being fully present in the moment. This honest sincerity builds on itself to form an authentic sense of community that combines capitalism's self-interest with socialism's sharing to form a new undefined ideology, neither left nor right, meeting somewhere in the middle or round the back. Although each family has its own unique livelihood, with considerable diversity of income levels, there is unwritten subliminal agreement that, rather than how rich or poor people are, it's enjoyment of the beauty and adventure of the place that counts. Because of this essentially green experience being its main foundation, the community could be considered an eco-village.

Although this new kind of village has the all-important central meeting place of a more traditional model, complete with even a public green space and direct and convenient public access, it is more spread out. Many of the folks live along the shorelines of the neighbouring channels, each with their own private dock and boats that link us all together. I have recently heard us all referred to as "the boat people."

Even the folks who live on the same island as the village centre and walk or drive off-highway vehicles to get there have had to travel by their own private boats to get to their island, there being no direct public road access. Although outboard motors are not green, they do connect the more remote homesteads with each other and with the village centre. Not all of the remote homesteaders within a five-mile radius of the community centre care to participate much in community affairs, but many do, and just about all the 100 or so year-round residents come to the village dock and post office at least once a week to collect their mail, which arrives three days a week by float plane.

A weekly market and lunch, held on the public dock on Wednesdays, brings people together in all kinds of weather to socialize, collect their mail and trade their produce. This event is also becoming a popular, unique tourist attraction in the summer-time. This helps the peripheral homesteads, like ours, to be more efficient through specialization and division of labour. For instance, we sell or trade our surplus eggs and seasonal vegetables there on a regular basis. The community market provides a bit of cash flow and welcome social entertainment, all of which contribute to strengthening the symbi-otic relationship between the homesteads and the community, making them both more sustainable.

A monthly newsletter greases the communication

wheels with information, debate, entertainment and intrigue. The soulful old buildings that were built by the hippies are now being used by their grandchildren. The bunkhouse, for instance, continues to function as a community centre and has recently been refurbished with a brand new kitchen extension. The old school building has been renovated and converted into a community woodworking shop. Both these projects depend largely on volunteer labour and donations of local materials, although some grants from governments and private charities have also been enlisted. On the write-up for grant applications, part of the stated "intended use" of the bunkhouse kitchen was the more humorous than realistic notion of teaching men how to cook, while the crafts shop was to teach women how to build.

A project I volunteered a lot of time on was building a new dock at the public road end access. This is the gateway to the outer islands if you are on the way out from town or the gateway to the rest of the world if you're on your way in. It's where we change out of boat mode into car mode and vice versa. The rough dirt public road, connecting as it does with the main provincial highways and ferries, was always there, but in the old days it was barely usable, and most town trips required a ten-mile boat ride which, in winter, was right into the teeth of the southeasters on their way up the Georgia Strait from Seattle. While contributing to all kinds of wild adventures, this also made life in the outer islands more dangerous, especially for those folks with marginal old boats. It was one more additional and expensive factor in whether people were able to hang in and remain in our area or not.

More recently the road was improved and a private float was installed which enabled boats to tie up and be left reasonably safely, and a few people started using it. The main catch was the 30-foot gap between the float and the shore. There was a makeshift raft on a pulley and the obvious unwritten understanding was to always pull the raft back to the float when you'd finished using it. Unfortunately, all too often some bozo gapped out and left the raft on the shore side so the raft got hung up on the rocks as the tide went out, resulting in the next users having to strip off and swim to get back to their boats after a tough day in town.

A few years ago our local regional district coun-cillor and I brokered a three-way partnership deal between the local government, a local fish farm and the local community to build a properly certified small boat dock for public pedestrian use. The local council would take over the lease, ownership and insurance and provide a grant for a new ramp; the private company would donate recycled galvanized steel and Styrofoam-billeted floats while the local community users would volunteer labour and materials for a new landing stage.

When at last, after years of bureaucratic contor-tions, we were ready to start construction, it was midwinter and we needed a really low tide so we could pour concrete pads for our pilings on the intertidal foreshore, but at this time of year the low tides are at night. So there we were at ten o'clock at night on the slippery beach with an icy northerly outflow wind blasting arctic cold air out of Bute Inlet from the Interior Plateau. We had generators running for floodlights and cement mixers, with a gang laying out forms, another carrying buckets of navy jack from a pickup truck at the bottom of the hill across the beach to the site and yet another mixing cement and wheelbarrowing it into the forms. With at least a dozen people working hard to keep warm the job got done, and just in time before the rising tide wetted our forms. We all dispersed into the blackest of winter nights, some of us bucking a huge flood tide to boot – quite a relief to get back home for a hot toddy and a warm bed!

This small project, though fraught with bureaucratic delays, was very rewarding in itself, serving as it does to make the outer islands more accessible to the public and the rest of the world more accessible to the islanders; it was a great boost to community spirit and the most successful of my experiences with the mainstream public process.

15

OFF-GRID HOMESTEAD

"What's your place like now?"

OUR HOMESTEAD IS THE HEART of our field of care and a good place to focus our conscious intention to consolidate our relationships with our environment. It occupies a two-acre clearing in the forest that opens out onto a mossy bluff overlooking the ocean. Most of the clearing is a grassy south-facing meadow with some recently planted fruit trees that have now become an orchard. We also have about half an acre of garden fenced off with an eight-foot-high cedar picket fence to keep the deer out.

At the back of the garden on the inland side we have a barn which is used for storing firewood, a chicken house, tractor shed, lumber storage and a workshop on the second floor. Behind the barn is a quarter-acre chicken run with a wire fence around and fish net over to keep the chicken hawks, owls, blue jays and ravens out.

Our old cosmic shack has long since been replaced by a proper house, occupying the same strategic spot on the bluffs overlooking the ocean: larger, more fancy and hopefully more durable. It has its own sewer gravity feeding down to a septic tank buried in the garden and out to a septic drain field in the meadow. We also have a small guest cabin, partially hidden in the trees behind the garden, with its own outhouse.

A small three-season stream flows out of a nearby swamp and down through our meadow before steeply descending the last forested slope to the sea. We modified the swamp by building a small dam and raising the level of the swamp to accommodate an intake pipe for a micro-hydroelectric Pelton wheel turbine that supplies almost all of our electricity during the eight winter months. For the summer months we have a bank of solar panels in the garden delivering power to our batteries in the house. If and when all else fails we have a small gasoline-fired generator backup. As well as powering our fluorescent lights, this homemade electricity enables us to operate satellite internet communications, telephone and TV.

A one-inch plastic pipe delivers gravity-fed clean, fresh water 1,800 feet from a surface well higher up on the mountain. We bring in propane in 100-pound tanks from town to supply gas for the kitchen cook stoves, refrigerators and domestic hot water systems.

Most of these "systems" evolved, step by step, by trial and error over a long period of doing what worked best and was affordable at the time. Now that we are much more conscious of the importance of relationship, we have come to understand how the ambience of the place is generated by the way the parts relate and support each other to form a whole that is more than the sum of the parts.

This organic process of relational holism echoes the natural world and literally brings life into our man-made environment. I am always pleased when visitors say, "Your homestead feels really good, the way it all fits together."

An example of the way the many parts of the homestead fit together in an interconnected web of smaller parts is the barn. Sawdust from the power tools in the workshop upstairs, above the chicken house, drops down and mixes with the chicken manure to enhance the compost, which enriches the soil in the garden. The health of the chickens and the yellowness and nutritional value of the eggs depend on greenery and grubs that the chickens find on their daily "open range" scratching rounds at the periphery of the meadow. The heat in our house depends on the spring-stacked firewood in the open-sided barn, protected from the rain but dried and ventilated by summer sunshine and warm westerly winds. Machinery, including the tractor and the ATV, their various implements and fuel supplies, also shelter under the wings of the barn close to the rough dirt roadways that ring the homestead and connect to the rest of the property. The covered workspace of the barn is also conveniently close to tools in the workshop above. Also nestled under the eaves of the barn roof are the satellite dishes for the communications and the internet systems in the house. They, in turn, are powered by the homemade electricity from the micro-hydroelectric turbine in the stream and the solar panels carefully positioned at the point of maximum sunshine in the garden. Underground cables deliver power, first to the batteries in the basement of the house and then back out to the barn and all the ancillary buildings. Similarly, all the different parts of the homestead are interconnected by the vital supply of water running from the well partway up the mountain down through branch lines buried in the ground to protect them from frost and wind chill.

One of our greatest joys and also one of our strongest assets is hospitality. We built our new house and garden bigger than we needed for ourselves because we love sharing our home with others, and the more time goes by and the more energy we invest in the place the more people seem to enjoy it. Also, as the world gets more hectic and artificial, people are starved for the peaceful ambience and silence that we take for granted, not to mention Laurie's sumptuous gourmet meals with fresh seafood and organic garden produce.

The ultimate goal is for the homestead to become more sustainable by strengthening both its internal and external relationships. So if, as well as making it more productive, we can entice the world to come and visit us, then so much the better. To this end we benefit considerably from hosting Wwoofers, young people travelling the world who are members of World Wide Opportunities on Organic Farms. They stay with us for a while and work in trade for their board and lodgings.

As the years go by, the aging process, not to mention health crises, increasingly limit our ability to do sustained physical work, so it really helps to have some youthful Wwoofers around to bring in the firewood or dig and weed the garden. The visitors in return have an opportunity to experience life in the bush and learn a few skills while at the same time engaging with the local people and their daily lives, as opposed to being mere spectators as are most tourists. Laurie always spoils them in the food department and we always offer them lots of time off work to hang out or go kayaking or hiking our local trails. We enjoy their youthful enthusiasm and seeing our place afresh through their eyes.

We once had a Wwoofer who was a Swiss banker on a mid-career sabbatical. He had deliberately chosen to spend time with farmers and get his hands dirty. He was very methodical and thorough, as one might expect, and applied himself well to the tasks we gave him. Of course, he spoke English very well too. For his day off, he announced he would like to kayak around our island. He had not had much experience so this was quite an ambitious challenge involving paddling solo 20 kilometres, through two sets of tidal rapids, in one day. He was fit and generally competent and had a very positive attitude, which we always considered the primary requisite for any outdoor adventure. Rather than discouraging him, we helped with his preparations and emphasized the particular importance of getting his timing exactly right to go through the rapids at slack water, and gave him a hand-held radio for emergency contact. When he was finally ready to leave he asked, very sensibly as usual, "Is there anything else I should know?"

"Well, only to expect the unexpected," I replied.

"What does that mean?"

"Anything might happen," I laughed.

"Like what?" he replied quite nervously.

"You might have a transformational experience," I laughed again.

"What on earth is that?"

"Don't worry about it. You'll find out if and when it happens. Good luck!" I waved goodbye.

He made it round the island without any significant trouble and back home in time for supper, very pleased with himself. We were suitably impressed and quite relieved. Next day, however, after work, he went paddling the kayak close by our place and came back home for supper in tears.

"What's the matter?" we asked, this time concerned ourselves.

"I saw a baby seal. It came right up to me." He sobbed breathlessly. "It rubbed itself against my kayak. I reached out and touched it. It had big round eyes that looked right at me. It was so beautiful. It stayed with me a long time. I took lots of photos," he panted.

"Aha," we laughed, "a transformational experience, no less!"

"How is Laurie's garden now?"

LAURIE'S PRIDE AND JOY, THE garden, is the heart of the homestead. Its central position and function generate the pulse of the whole place through a web of arterial connectivity. It too is made up of parts whose relationship with each other creates an organic and synergistic order (life) that generates the cohesive ambience of the whole homestead.

As well as keeping the deer and chickens out, the cedar fence around the garden provides a strong boundary that accentuates the sense of enclosure and security. It took us three years to build, and we used a cunning trick that combats the rotting of the wooden support posts where they are dug into the ground. Instead of using chemicals that would be harmful to other microorganisms, we torched the surface of the lower part of the cedar posts in a hot fire. Once we had the posts in place we salvaged cedar logs from the beaches and split them into rails and pickets. As well as being generally resistant to weathering, with a bit of skill and a mulling axe and wedges, cedar splits remarkably easily. A random arrangement of lengths for the pointed pickets confuses and discourages deer from trying to jump the fence.

The irrigation system is another important part of the garden that while fulfilling its essential function of watering the plants also adds life to the whole garden by relating all the other various parts together in a cohesive arrangement. It too has evolved through years of trial and error and hard-earned experience from its original version of a single pipe lying on the ground coming downhill from a well with a tap on the end to a complex, underground arterial web of branch lines, each with computerized valves that open and close at strategic times. In periods of prolonged drought that we sometimes experience in the late summer and fall, just when the plants are biggest and need most water, we have to ration and monitor the supply very carefully. Self-sufficiency requires that you be there to participate and take care of things, preferably before they go wrong.

"How much of your own food do you grow?"

PROBABLY ABOUT 60 PER CENT of our own fruit and vegetables, with a surplus of eggs, garlic and raspberries that we sell, trade or give away at the local market. Plus we eat quite a bit of locally caught fresh cod, salmon, prawns, clams, oysters and venison. We don't eat a lot of meat because of minimal freezer capacity. Even so, we spend a lot on dairy products and dry foods such as grains and pasta and still seem to have significant grocery bills in town.

Over the years we have learned which vegetables are best suited to our land, climate and storage capability, concentrating on the ones that give us most value for least effort. Some root crops such as carrots, parsnips, turnips and beets, as well as leeks and kale, so long as they are covered to protect them from wind chill, can best be stored by leaving them in the ground all winter. Onions and garlic are stored in the root cellar, where it is cool but not freezing. Bush and pole beans do very well in season but need to be canned for storage, though we also sell or trade our surplus at the weekly community market.

In the fall, we plant all the other plots that do not have winter crops, including the cold frames and greenhouse, with fall rye grass which continues to grow through the winter and is dug back over into the soil in the spring. This green manure, together with substantial amounts of compost, adds natural fertilizer to the soil, making it rich and black. Household scraps, grass clippings, sawdust, chicken manure, seaweed and cardboard, mixed in ventilated bins, assist the composting process. Weeding is done entirely by hand without the use of herbicides or pesticides.

All of the land area that is now the garden and orchard was originally cleared with our own hands and backs over a period of many years, from clear-cut logging slash. Visitors have been known to say, "You could have done all that in a week with a machine, you know!"

"But we had no machine, nor money to pay for it!!" And then, as if trying to convince ourselves, "Besides, it was fun and we did have some help from pigs!"

For many years we used gasoline-powered rototillers to cultivate the vegetable plots, but the machinery, even when bought new, did not last very long before it was more trouble and cost than it was worth. These days we dig all our plots at least once a year by hand, often with the help of Wwoofers.

If the garden were just about the economics of producing food a person could be excused for wondering whether the cost of the vast amount of labour that goes in is justified by the benefit coming out. For it to make as much sense as it unquestionably does for us, we have to accredit value to a number of other factors. The process of working the land can be therapeutic and meaningful in itself. Sometimes it's good to get your hands dirty and grab hold of nature instead of just watching it go by. It's another readily available way of being in the Zone, engaging ourselves with the energy of the land and nature. This source of happiness and meaning is the essential motivation and reward for our alternative lifestyle. We have known this for a long time, right from the start, and now we take it for granted, but a recent young Wwoofer, after spending a whole day digging over our garden, exclaimed excitedly, "That's one of the best days in my life! I had no idea that hard work could be so enjoyable!"

We have also always known the value of fresh organic and unpolluted food that tastes good. Again, visitors are constantly remarking on how good a raw carrot tastes, right out of the ground, or a fresh raspberry picked right off the bush. Plus the lack of herbicides, pesticides and genetic modification and the presence of mineral and vitamins – not to mention all the fresh air and exercise – are all very healthy. What mere numbers can possibly be put on such ethereal value?

To me the most priceless feature of all, the one that gives me the greatest and increasing pleasure, was expressed by the girlfriend of the above-mentioned Wwoofer, with whom I shared a very special moment, taking a break from working and sitting on a bench under a rose bush, reflecting and absorbing the ambience of our garden:

"This is like a sanctuary. It is so peaceful and harmonious."

**"How much of your electricity
do you generate yourselves?"**

ABOUT 95 PER CENT OF it. As mentioned earlier, we have a micro-hydroelectric Pelton wheel in the small stream that flows out of a swamp and down through our meadow for eight winter months and solar panels for the summer months. Very occasionally we have to use our gasoline-fired generator as backup.

We built a dam across the exit stream from the swamp and the laid 200 feet of 2-inch flexible PVC pipe along the ground down to the Pelton wheel turbine to the beach at the bottom of the hill. The pressure in the pipe forces water through a half-inch-diameter jet which squirts against an 8-inch-diameter hard plastic wheel that causes the wheel to spin. The mechanical power of the spinning shaft of this turbine is then converted to 12-volt electricity with a Ford truck alternator mounted on the shaft directly above the wheel. The 12-volt power runs through a control panel into thick wires lying on the ground that deliver it 150 feet up to the house.

An important component of homemade electricity is having a way of storing the power in a bank of batteries so it is available when you need it. The most common batteries are 12 volt, just like those in cars except bigger. Whereas a typical car battery is 80 amp hours, we bought an 800 amp hour battery. From the batteries the power is "inverted" to regular household 110 volts for distribution in the house circuits. An additional advantage of an inverter is that while it is delivering power from the batteries it can also receive power from an auxiliary gasoline generator and use it to charge the batteries when the Pelton wheel or solar panels are low.

As far as appliances are concerned the most important principle is that the more of them you have and the longer you have them on, the more power you need. Conversely, and perhaps this has become the greatest issue of our time, the less load (demand) we have, the less power we need (supply) and the less subsequent impact (footprint) on the environment. Perhaps even more succinct for the future is that the less power supply there is available, the less we are going to be able to use. Our small 120-watt turbine going 24 hours a day is enough for the modest load we require, which, though way more than what we had been used to, is still tiny compared to the average North American suburban household's uses (ten times smaller, in fact).

Any electric appliance that uses heat elements or moving parts consumes a lot more electricity than, say, lights or electronic equipment. So most of our requirements involve the latter, and the compromise we made was that for the large load appliances, such as washing machine, vacuum cleaner and power tools that are only on for a short time, we use the backup gasoline generator. This has an additional bonus of charging batteries at the same time.

Another important factor in reducing load requirements is that fluorescent light bulbs, and now LEDS, though more expensive than regular light bulbs, use one-fifth of the power of regular (incandescent) bulbs. They also last much longer. We purchased a lot of our equipment from an alternative technology outfit in California, and in the introduction to their catalog they claimed, "If the US government gave every household in the States fluorescent light bulbs, at a fraction of the cost of the first Gulf War (which was happening at the time), America could be an energy exporting country within five years."

Part of the advantage of our new system is that it has enabled us to have a reliable telephone, a computer and eventually a colour TV, all of which use relatively little power and provide a huge benefit, not least of which is the increased ability to "relate" with the rest of the world from our remote location.

16

ORGANIC HOUSE

"What happened to the old cabin
in the woods, the cosmic shack?"

WE TORE IT DOWN. THAT was not difficult. It
would have soon fallen apart anyway so we thought
we'd save it the trouble. It gave us the next 20 years'
supply of cedar kindling.

"What sort of a house do you live in now?"

WHEN GRADE 8 CAME ROUND and it was time

for Kiersten to go to high school in town, we tried several different scenarios, the first of which was renting a small house closer to town on the next island for the school year. So we too were forced to leave our beloved homestead on the outer islands for a while even though we came home every weekend and holidays. Fortunately the house we rented on Quadra had a few acres of pasture and some outbuildings so we were able to move Riskie the horse as well as Sheen dog, Tweedy the cat and the chickens.

This meant I had to take a job as a carpenter building custom houses, which turned out to be fun and enabled me to learn a lot. It also led to a significant improvement in our financial situation. At coffee breaks, on site, I would sit in on discussions about how the next pieces of wood were to go together and I would often do quick sketches with a carpenter's pencil on a scrap piece of plywood. When one of the builders, called Larry, saw one of these sketches he exclaimed as if surprised,

"Hey! You can draw!"

"Sure, I know how to draw," I answered. "I just don't know what."

"Why don't you do us some decent drawings then?" he said. "We'll tell you what to draw."

Larry talked his clients into paying me to do design and drafting work, and they taught me about the kind of information he required on a practical working drawing. He liked my drawings more than some of the other professional drawings (or sometimes no drawings at all) he was used to working with. To my surprise the clients were prepared to pay my modest fee. In this way, I stumbled across a specialty niche that enabled me to make more money than I was used to. Plus I could do the drawing work at home.

As well as providing an irregular but nevertheless significant cash flow, this new-found interest and skill I had acquired, building, designing and drafting custom homes, made me all the more dissatisfied with our old cabin in the woods. Apart from being altogether too shabby, its roof was starting to leak quite badly and was going to have to be replaced. It had served us well for 12 years, which was not bad for an average cost of $100 per year, but when it came time to replace the leaky roof we decided to scrap it and build a proper house.

To this end, we made a cunning trading deal with two logger friends up in the Homathko Valley at the top of Bute Inlet. They had reclaimed some large old-growth fir logs which had been used by a previous generation of loggers as bridge timbers across one of the big side rivers in the valley. The timbers were now washed up on the riverbank, tangled together by rusty old cables and spikes, and because the company did not want to deal with all the rusty metal in the wood, one of the loggers had permission to take these logs for his own use. He offered a three-way trading deal with me and another fellow who had a sawmill and a tugboat. No money was exchanged and we had enough high-quality wood to build and finish all three of our new houses. I did some drawings for both their houses, in trade for which I received a full logging truck load of old-growth fir logs. I then prepared a milling list that I gave to the mill guy, who bundled the logs and towed the bundles down Bute Inlet with his tugboat, dropping my share off on our beach. When the tide went out, we loaded the wood onto our tractor-trailer and brought it up to our barn, where we stacked it under cover to dry out for a year.

I had a design worked out for our new house that was quite simple and easy to build, but Laurie was inspired by a Frank Lloyd Wright book I had made the mistake of showing her. So as the house went up the design evolved into something more complex and sometimes very challenging to build, especially with primitive tools and my limited skills and budget. As well as getting all the timbers and framing material from local Bute Inlet wood, we made the roof from cedar shakes hand split from nearby forest, and all the external siding, fascias and trim are also from locally grown and milled cedar.

I had seen Larry demonstrate the importance of patience and enjoyment in the hands-on process of building in the timeless way, in the moment, the Zen of building.

"You have to slow down and focus your attention!" he said.

Practising this skill, rather than rushing ahead to get the job finished, was a hard lesson for me to have to learn until it dawned on me that this was an opportunity to apply the attunement that I had learned from the natural environment to the man-made environment of daily life. If there was something about the design or the way I had built it that did not feel right the first time, I learned to patiently take it apart and adapt it so it did feel right. Parts of our house were built three times over. Though not feasible in a commercial context, this way of building is a much more organic process in which the character (life) of our house evolved through a step by step process of experiential feedback from the situation rather than from the pure conceptualization of planning.

We have also made good use of the bluff, with the ocean view facing south, by locating the house directly onto the bedrock and using a split-level floor arrangement that nestles down a series of steps in the rock. The porch and entry area are accessed directly from a short driveway leading out to the bluff from the garden, barn and orchard areas. Our main bedroom and bathroom are also at this level. Half a level up from the entry, the open plan living room, dining and kitchen areas have a fine view through magnificent big fir and cedar trees to the channel and nearby islands below. Because the ground below falls away so steeply the deck, out front, is perched precariously high up in the trees.

A prominent feature in the great room is a stunning central fireplace from local granite built by an old stonemason friend from England. Much to our amusement, he was easily disgruntled:

"This damned granite won't do what I want it to, especially with these crappy tools."

He was used to much more cultured stonework in the old country and could not understand that we and everyone else round here just love the rough character of the granite and his work.

A loft, which I use as my office, is very well lit by large prow-shaped clerestory windows that also receive a lot of passive solar heat, and opens down into the living room. A full story below the great room and a half-level down from the entry is a utility basement area with two small guest bedrooms, a laundry area, a root cellar, a wood stove and a central masonry stack that goes right up through the house alongside the stone fireplace in the living room. This works as a heat sink which helps to keep the house warm even after the wood fire has gone out at night. It also absorbs and stores the passive solar heat from the clerestory south-facing windows in the loft.

We have tried to make both the internal and external relationships of the house as strong and varied as possible. Just as the house itself is one part of the homestead that contributes to the life of the whole place, so at the smaller scale each of the parts of the house, while relating to and reflecting the larger whole, is itself a cohesive arrangement of smaller parts (illustrating relational holism). Generous, convenient and open traffic flows connect and unify these separate parts into a harmonious flow of space that adds life and synergy to the whole house. The result feels good and looks like it belongs and blends into the moss-covered bluffs in an opening into forest, with a fine view of the ocean at the front. A strategic driveway connects it to the garden and the barn at the back, to other parts of the property and eventually down to the dock.

All this had to be paid for as we went along because, since our income was irregular, we could not get loans or mortgages from any bank even if we had wanted to, which we didn't. So it was all strictly a pay as you go, step by step process. This means it's all paid for once instead of twice or more, as would have been the case with a mortgage, and the house continues to evolve as time goes by. It has a kind of honest integrity that comes from the use of local material and from having the blood, sweat and tears included and interwoven with the great satisfaction of building our own nest within our own means.

One big difference between the old cabin in the woods and our new organic house, and a significant indicator on the upward mobility scale, was the indoor bathroom where the loo gravity feeds out to a septic tank and drain field that's buried out in the yard. I, of course, scorned the idea at first and swore I'd never use it but would be faithful to my meditation practice in the outhouse. Part of the argument in the bathroom's favour, which eventually convinced me of its necessity, was for our clients we were trying to attract to our wilderness tours at the time. We had once heard one of them say, with typical English humour, "My idea of a wilderness experience is having the window open when I go to the bog."

Needless to say, once the bathroom (the bog) was up and running I never used the outhouse again and just like everyone else have come to take the warm seat for granted. I must say, however, that – incurable romantic that I am – I do miss the old outhouse ritual, especially in a raging storm.

-17-

HEAVY WEATHER

"What were the most challenging
weather conditions you had to face?"

WE'VE HAD SOME TOUGH TIMES in the mountains, but by far the most scary adventures have been on the water.

In our early days, once a month or so, we had no choice but to boat the whole ten miles from our island into Heriot Bay for groceries, fuel and building supplies and take our chances with the mighty southeasters. Many of our boats were low-budget affairs and, if powered at all, often had cheap and old outboard motors that were notorious for breaking down. We all experienced some harrowing adventures, with many lessons being learned the hard way about riding the fine balance between sheer joy and sheer terror. Most of these ended happily with only minor damage to boats and egos, but unfortunately there have also been tragedies with loss of boats and lives.

One couple had a fine old sailboat and really enjoyed the thrill of sailing, or at least he did. They were sailing into a southeast blow one time, on their way into town, with the boat full of kids, and the husband was showing off how well the boat would sail and how brave and adventurous he was. Unfortunately, his wife did not always agree, especially when things got really rough as they did on this occasion. When a particularly vicious gust heeled the boat so far over that the rail was in the water, she went below and came out brandishing a carving knife and screaming hysterically, "If you don't back off I'll cut the damned jib sheets loose!"

In recent years, improvements of the road on

the next island and the opening of our community dock, together with better boats and motors, have removed a lot of the adversity, but southeasters can still be a force to be reckoned with. They are the predominant bad weather wind on the BC coast in winter. Though the wind speeds can be extreme, sometimes reaching storm and even hurricane force, they are typically more moderate and well forecast. Often referred to as the "Pineapple Express," an anti-cyclonic storm spins counter-clockwise around troughs of low pressure and packs warm, wet air from tropical regions across the Pacific Ocean from the southwest. Arriving on our coast and being confronted by a wall of high mountains, the spiralling vortex is squeezed upward and deflected toward the northwest. As the rising moist air cools it condenses, and the winds blow faster from the southeast and dump copious quantities of rain.

As these southeast storms roll up the 100 miles of open fetch of the Georgia Strait, all the way from Seattle, they accumulate seriously big seas, which are made even bigger by having to squeeze into the channels of the outer islands. An additional unique and spectacular local variable occurs when the southeast wind opposes the current of a big flood tide rushing in from the ocean around the top end of Vancouver Island and squeezing through the rapids between our islands. The resulting "wind against tide rip" kicks up steep and chaotic seas.

At the height of the biggest southeast storm we've ever had, when hurricane force wind speeds, recorded at a local lighthouse, were 70 knots and gusting more and all the ferries on the BC coast were cancelled, Laurie and I were watching a Jack Nicholson movie on TV. It was just before bedtime and we were getting quite spooked by the violence of the gusts that were shaking our house. Suddenly there was a horrendous crash and we both leaped off the couch. I thought for sure our roof had caved in and ran upstairs expecting to see a gaping hole. Laurie, smarter than me as usual, ran out of the basement door and found that the huge 400-year-old fir tree that used to stand beside our house had fallen, roots an' all – fortunately away from the house – but it had pulled the outside deck supports clean off the side of our house.

Having ascertained that there was no apparent

damage to the house itself and that there was nothing else we could do about it anyway, Laurie shrugged and said, "Oh well! Let's go back in to Jack for some comic relief."

Inside continental Canada people are used to very cold conditions in winter, but it is generally dry and cold. All they need are gloves, toques, thermal underwear and maybe a good down-filled jacket. Most of the time on the BC coast, winters are mild, wet and dull. All we need are oilskin rain gear and gumboots. However, a potential for dramatic variability exists in certain parts of the coast, when the intensely cold interior air spills down through the deep valleys of the Coast Range and collides with the intense wet on the coast to produce much more challenging survival conditions than either of the two elements on their own. The timing, diversity, complexity and intensity of the local mix are inherently unpredictable. This dramatic battle in the sky makes life more interesting for year-round residents of the outer islands and can often be a source of adventure eliciting our close attention and care, if not our horror and outright fear.

The day after the Jack Nicholson storm, in the late afternoon, I went over to the next island to pick up the mail. On the way over to the post office I noticed a westerly breeze and a swell picking up in the channel, which usually means an abrupt change in weather. It had stopped raining and turned quite cold. On my return trip the sky cleared very suddenly to reveal an amazingly spectacular display of bright orange light in the final rays of the setting sun. The storm and the dull grey gloom of the previous few days was suddenly replaced by intense sunlight and cheerful kaleidoscopic reflections dancing off the lively westerly chop. As I looked, the dramatic scene became the more vibrant, dazzling and brilliant, the sky quickly changing from orange to deep red. I couldn't help noticing how far south and how low in the sky the sun was setting. "Quite a winter solstice light show," I thought.

Then, before I reached the dock, with the last glimmer of daylight left, the sky quickly turned to dark, steel-grey blue and an ice-cold blast of north wind smacked my bare cheeks and froze my gloves solid as the air temperature instantly plummeted and the wind-chill factor increased dramatically.

"Bute Outflow!" I gasped as I hurriedly tied the boat to the dock and ran up the hill to the house in an attempt to keep warm.

This less frequent but vicious north wind blows out from mainland inlets when arctic high pressure conditions advance farther south than usual, sometimes over the whole of southwest BC and down into the States. This intensely cold, dry arctic air flow accelerates as it squeezes down from the Interior Plateau through the deep valleys and inlets of the Coast Range. By the time this air flow reaches the outer coast, the "Outflow" winds can deliver 100 mph, subzero blasts which pick up the damp ocean air and freeze it into devastating, icy maelstroms.

The interface, or battle line, between the cold, high pressure system and the warm and wet low pressure moves up and down the coast as the opposing forces recede and advance. The two huge elements are on quite different cycles. The arctic high, once established this far south, usually lasts a couple of weeks before receding and then perhaps coming back again later. The low pressure systems usually last only about 24 hours before dissipating inland, but they can stack up back to back in quick succession.

Sometimes, when both systems choose to advance at the same time, they can hold each other at bay, generating a sort of no man's land as in a military battle. Or they can merge together to form a northeasterly wind that dumps large quantities of wet snow. Depending on which system wins that particular round of the battle, the snow will either freeze solid and stay on the ground for days and even weeks, or it will turn to mush and wash away next day. The battle continues, on and off, through most of the winter in varying degrees.

We happen to live very close to the mouth of Bute Inlet, which has the most direct route from the interior, through the biggest mountains and glaciers in the Coast Range. So we are heavily influenced by perhaps the most intense outflow conditions on the whole BC coast, the notorious winter "Bute," one of the most serious winds any-where on the planet. Fortunately, we are relatively protected from the full brunt of the Bute's fury, where its effect dissipates as it spreads out away from the exit of the inlet. Nevertheless, we are close enough to be very familiar with protecting ourselves from the worst of the adversity. Water lines have to be kept running and covered by leaves and moss to protect them from the wind chill factor as well as the subzero temperatures. The driest firewood with the highest calorie content has to be reserved for these special occasions. Experience has taught us to make sure we have reserves of staple food provisions, enough to last several weeks if necessary, so we don't have to travel out to town.

That particular cold snap lasted two weeks, and though the days were brilliantly sunny, everything was gripped in ice. Storm force, 60-knot outflow winds blasted out of the mainland inlets with 20°F air temperatures and a further 20 degrees of wind-chill factor closing schools, downing power lines and stopping the ferries and buses all over Vancouver Island.

When it's that cold for so long we start becoming alarmed by the hole in the woodshed. Normally we let the wood stove go out at night and rely on the heat sink effect from the solid masonry chimney in the centre of the house to radiate warmth through the night. But a cold snap meant we had to stoke the fire at pee breaks during the night in order to keep ahead of the wind-chill factor. We couldn't afford to let the house cool off because it would take ages to warm it up again.

We were also concerned about our pond and hydroelectric system drying up or freezing up. Fortunately, the penstock pipe is well hidden in thick underbrush that is both insulated and pro-tected from the wind. It is at times like this that we really appreciate what a crucial role our homemade systems play in our life support. Thanks to our Pelton wheel and the satellites, we were able to stay online and keep in touch. My sister emailed from Vancouver where, in a power outage, they were huddled around candles and worrying about us running out of candles and not being able to get out to the store.

"Candles my butt," I replied, "We have every light in the place on."

Another time, we were coming home from Heriot Bay in *Quintano*, late in the afternoon with a load of building supplies and expecting Bute

Outflow conditions. We made sure we left well before dark, but by the time we secured the load there was a sharp, icy Bute wind blowing right on our nose. As we proceeded up the channel, the wind picked up and waves started crashing over the bow, sending clouds of spray, which instantly formed a layer of ice covering the decks and all my heaviest heavy weather clothing. With frozen beard and eyebrows, it was all I could do to steer the boat, peeping out from behind the shelter of the cabin. Laurie, Kiersten and Sheen dog fortunately stayed reasonably cozy with the stove going inside the cabin.

At the halfway point I took advantage of the shelter offered by a small bay tucked in behind a point to stop, make a brew of tea and change my icy, wet clothes. By the time we reached our dock, there was at least an inch of solid ice over the whole boat and the helmsman, who had been fighting for some time to stay warm enough to function, using as much willpower as on any of his toughest winter ice climbs in the Rockies.

It was now pretty well dark, so rather than unloading the building supplies right there and then, we accepted the welcoming gesture of a neighbour who lived close by the dock. "Looks like you could use a hot toddy. Why don't you come on in to my house? I've got some old barrel whisky."

Trouble was that to get the hot water for the toddy he first had to get his old hippie wood stove cranked up, and it turned out he did not have any good dry firewood. Being already so deeply chilled, instead of getting warmer I was actually getting colder by the minute, so after watching him struggle unsuccessfully for ten minutes without any progress, Laurie and I drained our whisky cold and neat, turned our head lamps on and headed back to the dock to unload the boat.

Even though our bay was largely sheltered from the howling Bute wind, there were still occasional gusts that would have made carrying sheets of plywood particularly challenging even for a sober, sturdy man. Now, I was not only lacking in mental concentration from hypothermia, I was also tipsy. When I arrived at what I thought was the top of the ramp, a gust of wind caught the sheet of plywood I was carrying and spun me around backward. Instead of backing straight up onto the landing,

I staggered to keep my balance, took a sharp left turn and fell ten feet down off the ramp, banged my back on the slippery rocks below and rolled over into the chuck. I managed to crawl out, soaking wet, with sharp pains shooting down my legs, crawl up the bank to the landing and limp back into the neighbour's house.

"Here! Have some more whisky!" he cheerfully offered.

This time I was smart enough to decline, but I was shivering uncontrollably and feeling pretty sorry for myself. The neighbour had managed to get the fire going but only just. The wood was sizzling and smouldering without putting out any heat. He and Laurie helped me strip off my wet clothes, bundled me on to a couch and covered me up with a down duvet before taking off to finish unloading the plywood, leaving me shivering to death on the cold couch.

Now I realized things were getting really serious. I thought of running on the spot but the shooting pain in my legs was enough to discourage any movement. I was familiar with both the symptoms and the consequences of hypothermia.

I knew it saps the very thing you need for combatting it, mental acuity, so I had to concentrate really hard to prevent losing focus. I also knew that to reverse the process of decreasing body core temperature, insulation is not enough; a victim needs heat, preferably direct contact with another warm body. At that moment the neighbour's daughter showed up and tried poking around at the fire. Well beyond politically correct decorum at this point, I asked, "Would you mind lying on the couch and snuggling up with me for a while to warm me up?"

I immediately felt the difference her body heat made and was soon able to pull myself together enough to make my way back home.

In recent years the outflow winds have not been as intense as they used to be because winter temperatures in the interior Chilcotin Plateau have not been as low. That's why the pine beetle infestation of the forests has been so extensive. Traditionally, long periods of −25°c temperatures used to kill the beetles and stoke the outflow wind on the coast. This pretty obvious manifestation of global warming means the Bute wind may not be as extreme as it used to be, but the outflow influence is still there and the battle in the sky still continues. Folks round here all know the Bute could and probably will come back with a vengeance any time it chooses.

-18-

FLIGHT OF THE IMAGINATION

"What has been your greatest inspiration?"

THERE HAVE BEEN SO MANY in the past, but perhaps the most inspiring experience of all for me happened recently.

In August 2011 a top class American rock climber and base jumper, Dean Potter, scaled the big rock face of Mount Bute at the head of Bute Inlet. He then jumped off the 9,200 ft. summit in a wing suit, making a three-minute, world-record-breaking human flight, like a flying squirrel, and landed in the valley 7,000 ft. below. *National Geographic* was there to sponsor and film this elite achievement. The beautiful film, called *The Man Who Can Fly*, was aired on American TV in March that year but was not shown to the Canadian public until August 2012, when we had the honour of presenting it our local community centres.

I was lucky enough to have been invited along as a local guide and storyteller on this exciting expedition because of my knowledge and experience of the history and geography of this relatively unknown wilderness area. Over my many years guiding in the area, I have enjoyed the extraordinary hospitality of the old Homathko logging camp located two kilometres up the river from the head of Bute Inlet which we had used as a base for our Ocean to Alpine wilderness expeditions into the Waddington Range. There have been many polite but skeptical loggers who have endured my cookhouse ranting and raving about the place in which I apparently was heard to say, "One day the world will discover this place and jumbo jet loads of people will be coming to see the awesome beauty and climbers will be lining up to climb the 6,000 ft. near-vertical granite face of Mount Bute."

As it turned out, one of those loggers was also a keen young climber from Squamish who returned a few years later with two buddies and made a very fine first ascent of the big face. Then another one of the three, Jimmy Martinello, heard, through the climbing grapevine, that *National Geographic* and Dean Potter were looking for bigger and better mountain faces to film their climbing and wing suit base jumping. He suggested they team up on Mount Bute.

Quite a bit of the 45-minute film is devoted to Potter developing the wing suit and preliminary training exercises for the Bute expedition, including spectacular ropeless climbing on the big rock walls of El Capitan in Yosemite and breathtaking tetherless high-line walking. The expedition team that assembled at the road end on Quadra Island, less than one kilometre from our home, included as well as Dean and Jimmy two other world-class climbers, two film directors and cameramen, another cameraman, a rigger, a sound man, Dean Potter's girlfriend, his dog Whisper and me.

For the 10 hour, 50-nautical-mile voyage up Bute Inlet, we boarded *Misty Isles*, a converted fishing schooner run by Michael Moore from Cortes Island. In perfect weather, the visitors were suitably primed by the increasingly spectacular scenery, climaxing with their goal – Mount Bute, towering dramatically 9,200 ft. above the mouth of the mighty Homathko River at the head of the inlet. Finally, at the first sign of human habitation they had seen all day, the team stepped onto the dock at their base of operations, tired but highly stoked by the long exposure to the powerful elements.

A warm welcome and hearty refreshments awaited their arrival in the reinvented, industrial/tourism Homathko Camp. In the morning, and for the next four days, bad weather prevented any progress on the mountain. Though it was a test of their patience, the team used the delay to pay respectful dues to the dramatic mountain and ocean environment, and to ground themselves, both individually and as a group. It was impressive to witness how much affectionate camaraderie they generated among themselves and how much interest, respect and admiration they showed for the local environment, history and customs, including me. They even took their hats off, as loggers were expected to do, when they came into the cookhouse. This pause in the activities provided ample opportunity for the team to hear about some of the rich local history and folklore as well as some of my own climbing and ski touring explorations of the Homathko country. Even more special for me were the intimate conversations about the deeper motivations and passions that drove their extraordinary achievements.

When the weather finally cleared, because of the bad weather delay they had no time for practice or trial runs. So, organizing entirely on sight as they went along, the cameramen filmed the four climbers making a very fast ascent of the upper part of this impressive near-vertical granite wall, set against a background of blue sky and a magnificent expanse of peaks and glaciers at the heart of the BC Coast Range wilderness.

Then they had to rig a platform for Dean to make his sensational historic jump and breathtaking three-minute flight to a meadow in the valley far below. The other jumper, Wayne Crill, in an emotionally charged moment of decision, that for me was a highlight of the film, declined to jump. This scene, providing authentic, intensely moving human drama, accentuated just how refined and carefully considered Dean's performance was.

"What do you think was Dean Potter's essential motivation in making this film?"

EVEN THOUGH THE FILM IS ostensibly about extreme sport, in the film Dean answers that question by saying, "The film is not really about breaking records. It's more about shifting perception, heightened awareness and extraordinary human power." In private conversation I heard Dean say he was interested in conveying the message that we all have the potential to extend the limits of our capabilities and get more out of life simply by letting go of the psychological and cultural constraints that prevent us from doing so. He wanted to share the sense of freedom that he experienced and encourage other people to stretch the limits of their own possibilities.

"Does he have any suggestions about how to let go of the fear that holds us back?"

IN THE FILM, WHILE WALKING a tightrope hundreds of feet above the ground in training for the Bute expedition, with no safety tether, confronting the limit of his own capability, he says, "I focus my attention on breathing, especially exhaling deeply from the abdomen, like meditation and yoga." Presumably the exhaling helps dismiss the fear. While climbing without ropes thousands of feet up on the vertical face of El Cap he also tells of how "I used to climb with aggression and fear. That only got me so far. Now I climb with love and passion."

The film also dramatically showcases the rugged beauty and unmatched scale of the mountains soaring high above the turquoise mix of glacial rivers and ocean waters at the head of Bute Inlet that, as I've said earlier, I once heard described as "one of the world's best kept secrets, Canada's Grand Canyon, except bigger and better!"

It was this extreme verticality that attracted Potter as a suitable place to push the precarious and breathtaking limits of three extreme sports. So finely and with such intense drama and emotion is the line being drawn between life and death that the film also challenges the audience by stretching the limits of human perception in what Potter, very articulately, refers to as a "flight of the imagination."

In addition to all of this, the film succeeds in capturing what struck me so vividly from my experience of spending time with these world-class athletes, which was the extraordinary manifestation of the power of love. It showed in their camaraderie, their respect for local people, their overt passion for their chosen vocation and its wilderness environment and the sheer joy of living and, ultimately, in their truly remarkable stretching of human capability.

A tragic sequel to this story is that Dean Potter was killed recently during a squirrel suit flight in Yosemite. Although I don't know the details and can't be sure, my guess is that Dean's attention was distracted by the possibility of the park rangers waiting to arrest him on landing in the Yosemite Valley floor, where base jumping is illegal. To be less conspicuous required jumping at dawn or dusk when there are unfortunately more erratic up and down drafts. As well as facing a possible jail sentence Dean had taken on the political challenge of fighting to have the law changed, which must have entailed a significant load on his subconscious mind. In the high stakes game Dean was playing, there was no room for the slightest intrusion of subconscious distraction from absolute focus of consciousness in the moment.

-19-
THE LEGEND OF KAYAK BILL

"What happened to Kayak Bill?"

WE HEARD ABOUT BILL'S TRAGIC suicide in a surprise phone call from his ex-partner Lori Anderson in Sointula on Malcolm Island. She told me she was organizing a memorial service in their community and asked me to spread the word to as many of Bill's old climbing friends in the Canadian mountaineering community as possible and invite them to the wake.

When the wake was in full swing there were more than a hundred people present, which was not altogether surprising, because in spite of his hermit lifestyle, Bill had lots of friends. What was surprising and very mysterious, however, was the fact that very few of these people knew each other. Bill's ex-wife, Lori, had loosely facilitated a formal process in which she invited various people that she knew had known Bill well and asked them to tell their stories of their friendship with him in a somewhat chronological order.

A definite pattern soon emerged showing that even though Bill, being such a lovable guy, always made friends wherever he went, he also kept moving on and leaving old friends behind, just like he did with me. Furthermore, he never told his new friends very much about his previous life, so none of approximately half the people present who were from the coast had any idea who all these other folks from Calgary were, or that they represented the cream of Canadian mountaineering. "Billy the Bolt," as he was known to them, was a living legend on the other side of the Rockies. Of course, these Calgarians knew very little of the details of the west coast legend of "Kayak Bill." Even his more recent friends on the upper coast knew few of us old lower coast friends from earlier times.

This dramatic saga was heroic and tragic right from the start. Bill's childhood friend Perry Davis told how he became close buddies with Billy Davidson in an orphanage in Calgary where Bill's mother had dropped him, aged 9, and his younger brother and sister off on the steps and walked away from them. They never saw her again. They kept in touch with their father but he was unable to cope as a single parent. Something similar had happened with Perry and his sisters. Apparently, the orphanage encouraged the kids to follow their own interests. This explained why Bill could barely read or write but was a genius with electronics. In his early teens he built a robot that won a national award. It required him to go to Ottawa and have some VIP put his medal into the hands of the robot. The robot then walked across the room and delivered it to Bill.

Perry and Bill soon started hiking in the mountains together, and Perry described how Bill took to mountaineering right away and soon left him behind as he quickly became a very good climber and made all kinds of new friends, including members of the elite hard-climbing and hard-drinking Calgary Mountain Club. Prominent among these was the next speaker, who described how Bill soon developed a high degree of proficiency in the specialized skills required for climbing extremely steep and scary rock faces. His forte was solo climbing, which is particularly serious and scary. Another younger Calgary Mountain Club member told how, at a still very young age, the two of them went down to the rock climbing Mecca, California's Yosemite Valley, where Bill became the first Canadian-born climber to reach international fame by doing a very early ascent of the hardest and most scary big wall rock climb in the world. Soon after that, I met them there in those hazy, crazy, lazy days of warm California Indian summer.

When it was my turn to speak, I told the story of our pact, how we spent increasing amounts of time living out in the mountains and how after spending a large part of a day up a tree at Dick

Pearson's tipi, talking to the birds, Bill sold all his climbing gear, his motorbike and all his filming equipment and bought himself a bow and arrow and a leather outfit and took off into the Rockies to live off the land. Soon after I moved to the coast, Bill came out for a visit and we did our big trip up Toba Inlet together. On that trip I introduced him to painting and drawing. When I bought into the land co-op, Bill bought himself a kayak and paddled off into the wilds of the BC coast.

Others then picked up the saga of how Bill committed himself to the coast and managed, with admirable ingenuity and discipline, to support himself for the rest of his life living off the land and sea. He shunned the use of money and motor cars and trained himself in the use of wild edible plants, learning a lot from the Native people. His unique and total absorption in the coastal landscape was reflected in his paintings, which he used as trading items for the few trappings of civilization he needed such as tobacco and peanut butter. He moved farther out up coast each summer and set up primitive temporary driftwood base camps as he went. He was extremely strong and fit and could paddle phenomenal distances in a day if he cared or needed to. In winter he would retreat to remote communities and build a beechwood shack in someone's yard and work and play on his home synthesizer made from used radio parts. Otherwise he carried all his possessions in his kayak.

One person told us about Bill's enthusiasm for eulachon grease, a foul-smelling concoction made by the First Nations from rancid fish. He claimed it was especially helpful in combatting the cold coastal damp. One time he paddled his kayak up to the top of Knight Inlet to score some grease from the Natives. He was hoping to make a trade for some berry leather he had made and was giving his sales pitch to an elder, explaining how the berries would provide all the vitamins they needed for the winter. The old Native looked at him and smiled.

"Why don't you just make wine?" he asked. "Then you get your vitamins and you get pished as well."

Some of the later speakers at the wake, who had

spent time with him more recently, mentioned that Bill had been having some health problems, especially with his teeth. Friends had offered to help pay for treatment and yet Bill stubbornly refused to accept help or go anywhere near a doctor or dentist. This perspective inevitably led to the dramatic conclusion of the saga, the unanswered mystery which was now at the forefront of everybody's mind.

"How or why could anyone who loved life so much and was so well loved, possibly have taken his own life?"

Although Lori and their son Westerly did not speak publicly at the wake, I later had a chance to chat at great length with them in private. From our conversation and our comparing of notes we pretty well agreed on a possible answer to that mystery. To do so we had to indulge in some amateur common sense psychology. Against what must have been tremendous emotional trauma from the rejection of his mother, Bill's seemingly casual and laid-back manner disguised a steel-hard emotional defence mechanism that explained both his extreme self-reliance and his extreme reluctance, amounting to incapability, for long-term, deep emotional attachments. Lori confided that this trait was compounded in mid-life when they had agreed to go their separate ways. This amounted to another emotional rejection, which served to compound Bill's self-reliance.

Then Westerly told me that in his teenage years Bill tried persuade him to join him on his trips. Though Westerly enjoyed the lifestyle for a while, he decided it was not his path. Once again, apparently, Bill took this very hard, effectively seeing it as another rejection. Bill's response, as was his habit, was to move on even farther out.

If this hypothesis is true, then it's just a short stretch of the imagination to see that Bill, having experienced the effects of his body failing and facing the prospect of old age dotage, complete with dependence on other people or, even worse, society's institutions, chose instead what for him would be the logical, consistent, courageous and honourable way out, the way of the Samurai warrior.

So, now being the only one of the four original pact members who has survived to tell the tale, I have come to agree with John Donne: "No man is an island entire of itself. Therefore never send to know for whom the bell tolls; It tolls for thee."

WHIRLPOOLS IN THE TIDE

"What has nature taught you about what it means to be human at this time?"

NOW, WHENEVER I CATCH MYSELF worrying about the world, even though there is more to worry about than ever, I take a deep breath, look out of my living room window and watch the whirlpools unfolding in the flow of the tidal rapids. They gradually emerge from the spinning effect of the current boundaries between the main flow and the back-eddies and momentarily adopt a distinctive form and character before quickly enfolding themselves back into the flow of the main current. Their existence as separate entities, like our individual selves, is momentary if not illusionary; their individual character and behaviour, a mere ripple in the great flow of the tide of life.

Then, amazingly, approximately every six hours, the tide itself changes course and flows the opposite way, just another ripple in an even bigger swirling fluctuation of universal energy, all of which seems to know exactly what it is doing; energy fields within energy fields; knowingness within knowingness; universal consciousness.

Even though the whirlpools undoubtedly play a part in determining the specific unfolding of the current, unlike human beings they don't try to control it.

> "Does that not suggest that
> we have no free will?"

NOT EXACTLY. RATHER IT SUGGESTS that our will is more likely to be manifest and sustained when it resonates directly with the surroundings, thereby supporting that particular environment's ability to play its part in the whole continuity of life. Then our consciousness becomes one with the life-sustaining will of non-local or universal consciousness.

"What exactly is universal consciousness?"

IN MY MODEST UNDERSTANDING OF science, at the turn of the 20th century a fundamental disagreement existed in physics as to whether light was made of particles or waves. The famous double-slit experiment of quantum physics proved not only that it was potentially both but also that the particles themselves were choosing which aspect (particle or wave) would materialize at any particular moment. As well as being individual entities, subatomic particles can also simultaneously be waves of possibility in a background field of potential energy. Different particles have varying degrees of inclination to one aspect of their split personality or the other and even seem to pop back and forth, from one to the other, depending on whatever else is going on around them, including whether or not they are being observed.

When energy systems interfere with each other, waves of similar frequency (in phase) overlap and resonate, forming waves of higher amplitude, while those with dissimilar frequencies (out of phase) cancel each other out. The higher energy harmonic convergence of their wave functions enables each of the subatomic particles to know what the others are doing. The influence of the relationship spreads instantaneously and indeterminately throughout a background field of potential possibilities. Like birds in a flock or fish in a shoal all turning together at the same time, or young lovers merging together, their individuality is enfolded into relationship. Not only do the parts behave like a whole; they become whole. Particle aspect is the material thing that does the relating and wave aspect is the relationship.

Individual phenomena are only significant in the way they contain and reflect the whole and vice versa. Just as easily, wave aspect can and does (for whatever reason, including being observed) unfold back out of the background field into individual material form. This continuous synergistic relationship of parts knowing how to contribute and reflect larger wholes constitutes the background field of universal consciousness: Relational Holism.

> A World in a grain of sand ...
> Eternity in an hour.
>
> —Blake

"And what does this all mean for society at this time?"

NO DOUBT MY UNDERSTANDING OF this mysterious and highly elusive subject is exceedingly sketchy, and even the physicists have trouble articulating the precise implications, but there seems to be a consensus that when we observe or measure reality we change it. Furthermore, how we change it depends, among other things, on the attitude, state of mind, intention and belief of the observer. In some significant degree, we participate in creating our own reality. It seems that discordant frequencies in the energy field of our attitude, such as anger, dominance or judgment, encourage particle types of response in the energy fields of our surroundings. Harmonious vibrations in our attitude, such as empathy, partnership or listening, encourage wave types of response in our surroundings. So we should be very careful what we wish for and what we choose to believe.

"And what do you choose to believe?"

AFTER A LIFETIME OF EXPERIENCE living, working, playing and reflecting close to nature I believe that I am made of essentially the same material as the rest of the universe (star dust) and my body/mind duality is a reflection of its quantum wave/particle duality. The atoms and molecules of my brain and body are the particle aspect of myself and my mind is the wave aspect – the relationship I have with my internal and external environments. The "I" that I am is the ever-present observer of the internal dialogue between all my quantum sub-selves with their fluctuating boundaries, which sometimes exert their own identity (particle aspect) and sometimes relate and merge with each other and with my social and natural surroundings (wave aspect). The more integrated, balanced and calm ("together") the energy frequencies of my sub-selves are, the more correlation there is between the outside world and my inner feelings, mood and imagination, the wave aspect of myself. The more open and clear my body/mind is, the more access I have to and the more I am empowered by the unified wisdom of universal consciousness in the surrounding natural environment. It resonates directly with my inner feelings, telling my cells how to behave and how to be. This phenomenon is most powerful and evident in pristine wilderness.

> One impulse from a vernal wood
> May teach you more of man
> Of moral evil and of good,
> Than all the sages can.
> —Wordsworth

This internal and external attunement could explain what board riders and climbers mean by the "Natural High" and "being in the Zone." When we answer the call for adventure, follow our bliss and ride the wave of uncertainty, it seems the universe opens its doors of possibility to us. When we are so present in the moment, so in tune with ourselves and our environment that the surfer becomes the wave or the climber becomes the mountain, we are possessed of performance-enhancing confidence and a euphoric sense of unity and love. The overall experience dramatically extends our limits of what is possible. We discover that our true self (our soul) is something much bigger than we had previously been led to believe – part of the spontaneous evolution and natural selection of life. This could account for the three truly extraordinary events of my life: climbing the Nose of El Capitan, helping to save BC Parks and surviving a dissected aorta. It might also explain why we climb mountains.

The main obstacle to allowing this expansion of self to occur and maximize our potential capabilities, both individually and collectively, is inappropriate cultural conditioning. In order to procure agreement among large numbers of people, human cultures have created stories, legends, myths, belief systems, ideologies, religions, cosmologies, paradigms and mindsets. These imaginary mental constructs (maps of reality) have induced specific subconscious and automatic behaviour patterns to protect people from familiar hazards in their environment (the territory). These collective strategies have traditionally been very successful in keeping tigers and enemies away from our homes and fingers away from fires. They have also allowed massive increases in population, especially in recent years. An extraordinarily high percentage of contemporary behaviour is now considered to be automatic subconscious conditioning. Driving cars is a classic example.

When confronted with rapid and unknown changes in the social and natural environment, however, these programmed responses can easily become obsolete and dangerously counterproductive. Civilizations have collapsed because they failed to adjust their beliefs (myths) to drastic changes in the environment that they themselves had created. This is increasingly the case in modern society, where vested interest in the status quo is preventing necessary adaptation to rapid technological, social and climatic changes. Brainwashing and subconscious propaganda on the grand scale enforce the prevalent mindset that we are individual objects, separate from and superior to each other and the rest of the world. We can therefore extract, reduce and modify (rape and pillage) the world to suit our ever-expanding need and greed without any cost to ourselves. We are led to believe that pursuit of wealth and instant gratification are the singular sources of meaning in our lives; reality exists out there regardless of what we think or do; we are powerless to do anything about it so what does anything matter; individual self is all that we are – our true self. Consequently the mainstream culture of contemporary civilization is stuck in the adolescent stage of development (ego), incapable of accepting adult responsibility for its relationship with other beings and the rest of the planet. We are in danger of creating an artificial, soulless, fragmented and violent world that is sadly devoid of both conscious brain power and the instinctive ability to survive – ironically, the very attributes that are supposed to have made us superior and separate in the first place.

It's not that particle reality is wrong and wave reality is right; both can and do happen simultaneously all the while, like yin and yang, two sides of the same coin, possibly correlating to two sides of the brain. In everyday life the wave aspect of self can bring meaning and joy to our lives. Most of us are in some degree empowered by our relationships with others and our internal and external environments, as evidenced in the arts, sport, sex, imagination, intuition and the placebo effect. Similarly, other creatures such as salmon and pigeons find their way home, and elephants break their chains and run uphill to avoid tsunamis. But because wave aspect energy is subtle and interacts with our subjective reality and is therefore indeterminate and cannot be measured, it does not fit into the dominant objective and mechanistic cosmology of the official contemporary belief system and has been largely marginalized and ignored. However, to fully know who we are, to fulfill our potential and to survive the challenges we face, we must redress the particle/wave imbalance by consciously reasserting the critically important wave aspect of our being.

"How do we do that?"

IN ANCIENT AND ABORIGINAL CULTURES, rites of passage (vision quests, walkabouts and heroic journeys) deliberately exposed individual adolescents to the fear and uncertainty of wildness with minimal cultural protection – to face whatever reality actually exists out there as opposed to what is supposed to be. This challenge required initial courage to honestly confront the demons in both the external and internal environments, but once committed to, it invoked the fight or flight response. This fundamental survival instinct short-circuited subconscious cultural conditioning, heightened awareness and provided extraordinary physical capability. The transformational experience of overcoming the adversity (slaying the demons, climbing the mountain or finding the way out of the labyrinth) inspired visions or stories to take back to the tribe. Once interpreted by the elders, these new visions and stories helped the prevalent culture adapt to ongoing changes in the environment.

It's quite possible that "high risk" sports and adventure education are modern substitutes for these ancient rituals and have some effect in mitigating the self-destructive degeneration of society. Unfortunately the transformational wave aspect of the stories are all too easily and often co-opted by the particle aspects of measured competition, egotism and litigation. Plus the wilderness, the source of so much of the inspiration, is rapidly being diluted and tamed.

A simpler way of manifesting the wave aspect of reality is by practising mindfulness. Paying conscious attention in general and focusing on breathing in particular, we can put the particle aspect of ourselves on hold and experience directly the essential relationship between our external and internal environments (wave aspect). As well as alleviating suffering by helping to reduce habitual craving for something different from what actually exists (as in Buddhism), this connection opens our body/minds to the consciousness of the environment, allowing it to guide our behaviour toward the critical path of natural selection and spontaneous evolution of life.

I have been teaching mindfulness as a way of staying safe and staying found in the mountains for many years. Now Parkinson's disease is forcing me to practice more diligently what I have been preaching – conscious awareness of my body movement, such as coordinating the rhythm of arms and legs and very careful choice of where to put my feet. When I am tired and not paying attention I stoop, drag my right foot and don't swing my arms: the classic Parkinson's shuffle. By paying conscious attention, I can walk quite normally. This requires a huge amount of mental effort and discipline. It can be significantly assisted by loving support.

I believe mindfulness happens and can be encouraged to happen more often in the less extreme circumstances of everyday life, whenever we are relaxed enough for our body/minds to openly and unconditionally engage with the ambience of our surroundings. This could explain those magical moments that make life more meaningful and joyful: an infant's smile; a lover's touch; creation and appreciation of art, music and dance; a cat purring on our lap; a decent conversation or a good belly laugh – when we are fully present in the moment and experiencing unconditional love.

"How can mindfulness help change the world?"

IT SEEMS THE HUMAN RACE is at a critical crossroads. For our species to survive we must abandon the brainwashed allegiance to obsolete and erroneous imaginary mental constructs of reality which perpetuate increasing centralization of wealth, atmospheric pollution and destruction of biodiversity. Only then can we commit ourselves, both as individuals and collectively, to engaging with and being partners in the self-regulating evolution and interconnected flow of life. A new understanding of who and what we are is required: a new paradigm, a new cosmology, a new and more accurate map of reality that will bring us closer to the mystery of the truth.

The realization that we can and do create our own reality empowers each individual to choose what kind of world we want and requires us to be more consciously aware of the consequences of our behaviour. Increasing the wave aspect of our being and maximizing our capability to survive requires that we allow mindfulness to happen between our thoughts and our actions. We need to slow down enough to practise looking before we leap, with more carefully considered decisions and less automatic, compulsive and blind regurgitation of ideology and self-righteous condescension. We are all entitled to our own beliefs, but we can never be so sure that our truth is "the truth" that it gives us the right to impose it on others. In the new holistic paradigm, mutual respect fostering diverse and complex beliefs that resonate in symbiosis with the social and natural surroundings are more likely to lead to the truth. The way we consciously choose to relate to the other is a reflection of our own truth. We should do as we would be done by.

With governments abdicating their social contracts to protect citizens, people are finding more direct ways to confront the dangers of pollution, discrimination and oppression. Substituting creative work and recreation that is more mindful of being in this place and this moment could provide a cheaper, more effective and less environmentally damaging alternative to material aggrandizement as a source of meaningful happiness. Mindfulness is rapidly becoming more popular and is even being taught in schools. Can it catch on in time to produce a more accurate, relevant and sustainable map of reality? A web of interconnected, dynamic relationships rather than separate things? Being and becoming rather than doing, having and getting? Living, working and playing with nature rather than against her? Accessing and maintaining the critical path of survival of our species?

Far from surrendering personal freedom, by enhancing our partnerships with each other, with other species and with the earth itself, we could address the very real dangers we face as a species and redirect our destiny toward a more equitable and sustainable eco-centric (rather than egocentric) future. The increased sense of well-being and fulfillment from knowing ourselves to be a part of a far greater entity than ourselves could far outweigh the loss of individual aggrandizement and help us transcend the violent forces of tribalism and nationalism. Then the collective organism of Humanity might grow out of its adolescent and self-indulgent stage of development into more soulful, responsible and conscionable adulthood. Rather than fighting about which fictional order has the right and capability to control the world, we could focus our conscious attention on evidence of the very real and infinitely wonderful order that already exists. Like whirlpools in the tide, we might learn to play a small part in the spontaneous evolution of the community of creatures and plants that contribute to the magnificent living whole we call the planet Earth. We might realize the far higher potential of rediscovering where we belong – that nature is in fact our home and in nature we are at home. We are nature. We are not separate or superior.

"More cobbler, anyone?"

ROB WOOD has been a professional architect, pioneering mountaineer, organizer of ocean-to-alpine expeditions, instructor of wilderness self reliance at Strathcona Park Lodge and a founding member of the Friends of Strathcona Park, a protest group that helped stop logging and mining in the park. He and his wife, Laurie, still live on Maurelle Island, British Columbia.